CLASSIC
TOWN · PUBS
A CAMRA GUIDE

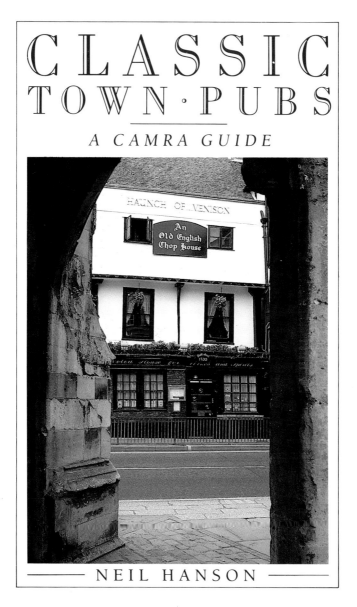

NEIL HANSON

Photographs by Mike Golding

PAVILION
MICHAEL JOSEPH

Classic Town Pubs went to press before the
government's proposed legislation on the relaxation
of pub licensing hours reached the statute book.
The hours given were correct at 1 January 1988,
if the law is changed, those hours should be
the minimum that the pub will be open;
if in doubt, telephone the pub!

First published in Great Britain in 1988 by
Pavilion Books Limited
196 Shaftesbury Avenue, London WC2H 8JL
in association with Michael Joseph Limited
27 Wrights Lane, Kensington, London W8 5TZ

Designed by Andrew Barron Associates
Photography by Mike Golding
Cartography by Reg Piggott

British Library Cataloguing in Publication Data
Hanson, Neil
Classic town pubs: a CAMRA guide.
1. Hotels, taverns, etc.— Great Britain
— Guide-books 2. Great Britain —
Description and travel — 1971- — Guide-
books
I. Title II. Campaign for Real Ale
647'.9541 TX950.59.G7

ISBN 1-85145-182-X

Printed and bound in Spain by
Graficas Estella

The photograph on page 3 is of the Haunch of Venison, Salisbury

CONTENTS

PREFACE

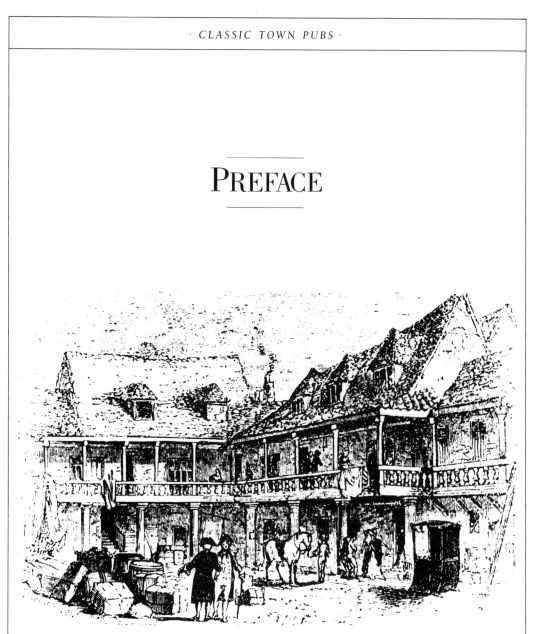

The Tabard at Southwark, the starting point for Chaucer's pilgrims on their way to Canterbury

There are over 70,000 pubs in Great Britain; some are palaces, some are hovels, but all are instantly identifiable by the term 'pub'. Despite the attempts of some breweries to impose corporate images upon them, pubs largely remain as idiosyncratic and individual as the people who drink in them.

Pubs reflect the regions and communities they serve: a boozer in Berwick is obviously different from a hostelry in Hampstead, but there are also common factors in the design, history and development of our town pubs which separate them from their country cousins. The lay-out, character and atmosphere of a country pub is often little altered from that of centuries ago, but, while there are town pubs with pedigrees as long, most have undergone a series of transformations reflecting the industrial, commercial and social changes in the development of our towns and cities.

The companion volume, *Classic Country*

Pubs, is a journey around rural Britain, calling in at some of our finest country pubs along the way; *Classic Town Pubs* travels to some of our great historic towns and cities, pausing to reflect on their past, present and future in one hundred superb town and city pubs.

Classic Town Pubs takes the form of a series of journeys from London, following routes through areas that have all played their part in the formation of present-day Britain. Roads used by Chaucer, Shakespeare, Pepys and Dickens; towns where invasion forces landed and where great battles were won and lost; Celtic, Roman, Anglo-Saxon and Viking settlements; cities that grew up around our great cathedrals, castles, and universities; medieval towns where the Guilds grew and prospered; ports which handled the goods of the world; the towns where the industrial revolution was born and its northern heartlands where the wealth of nineteenth-century Britain was created; and our great capital cities: Belfast, Cardiff, Edinburgh and, above all, London, once the heart of an empire, still a great financial and business centre. All these are steeped in history and traditions that can be understood and appreciated as easily in the pubs that developed alongside them as anywhere.

In these pages you will find the whole spectrum, from ancient coaching inns to city taverns, Victorian gin palaces to back-street boozers. To choose just one hundred out of the thousands of town pubs is a certain recipe for a classic pub argument! No reader will agree with all my choices, some may not agree with any, but I hope they will stimulate you to a few discoveries of your own and to some reflection on the central role our inns, taverns and pubs have played in the daily life of our nation.

They have survived the ravages of time and the depredations of developers, but often only because individuals and communities were prepared to fight for them. The magnificent Black Friar still exists to delight Londoners and visitors alike because a small group of people, led by Sir John Betjeman, set out to challenge the demolition order upon it.

As well as its tireless Campaign for Real Ale, CAMRA fights to save many other fine pubs from a similar fate at the hands of developers and insensitive architects and designers, for it is not necessary to demolish a pub in order to destroy it. CAMRA campaigns to keep the great British pub, serving great British beer, alive and well for us all to appreciate, not just as a piece of history, but as the living embodiment of a tradition that has been at the heart of British life for centuries – and that's something we can all drink to!

ACKNOWLEDGEMENTS

All books require the labour of many more people than the one whose name appears on the cover; this one is no exception. Roger Protz and Tim Webb have drawn deeply from their accumulated store of pub wisdom, and have given invaluable help with research and writing.

Mike Golding has completed the same long and arduous journey as myself, although he was excused a tour of duty in Belfast, and I am grateful to Paul Carter for the photograph of the magnificent Crown Liquor Saloon there. Andrew Barron has done both text and pictures more than justice with another classic piece of design.

I am grateful to Colin Webb, Viv Bowler and Margaret Nairne at Pavilion Books for their advice and support. My colleagues at CAMRA, Jill Adams, Jo Bates, Carol Couch, Iain Dobson, Clare Dockree and Malcolm Harding, helped to see the work through to the end in various ways and were always available to buy their rounds whenever the lure of the local overcame the call of the word-processor.

A book such as this can do no more than scratch the surface of the history and development of the pub. For more detailed study look at *The Traditional English Pub* by Ben Davis (Architectural Press) and Mark Girouard's *Victorian Pubs* (Yale). My own research was greatly assisted by George Williamson, who provided much helpful advice and information.

Lastly, three dedications: one to the many remarkable pub landlords and landladies without whom there would be no classic pubs, with commiserations to those less successful ones who have found it impossible to work one hundred hours a week and still smile; one to Swaledale – no better place, no better people; and one to Graham and Marilyn, who have discovered that New Zealand has everything that anyone could ever want . . . except a decent pub!

Opposite: The fine art nouveau tiles in Bennet's Bar, Edinburgh

INTRODUCTION

Inns, Taverns & Alehouses

We tend to use the terms 'inn', 'tavern' and 'public house' interchangeably, but all were at one time different types of pub serving different needs.

Inns were the forerunners of hotels, developing out of the old monastic hospices and offering travellers food, drink and a bed for the night. They stood on trading routes in villages and towns, and the country in between, and sold wine, spirits and ale. Inns were also customarily built alongside churches to house and refresh the construction workers, for church-building was a lengthy operation, taking several years; in the case of cathedrals, decades or even a century might be needed to complete a building.

Though many customers were strangers, inns were also used by local people as meeting places where deals could be struck, payments made and jobs sought and offered. Agricultural workers were hired at inns, farmers and market traders met to haggle over prices and groups of workers, such as miners, fixed contracts and divided their pay there.

Taverns were to be found in the few towns and cities that existed in pre-industrial Britain and particularly in London. They sold wine and food rather than beer, in surroundings that reflected the prestige and importance of their customers: merchants and bankers meeting for business as well as social reasons. Taverns were valued for their exclusivity; when the nineteenth-century, upwardly mobile, middle classes began to invade the hallowed precincts, many of the former customers retreated to the private world of the gentlemen's clubs.

As the cities grew, and new drinks like tea, coffee and chocolate became available, coffee and spirit shops and restaurants emerged to compete with the taverns. The atmosphere in these new drinking places was very much cooler than the warm and noisy alehouses and taverns,

Opposite: A detail of the superb tiling in the Golden Cross, Cardiff

A fifteenth-century brewhouse. Though the brewing equipment nowadays is a little more sophisticated, the art of brewing remains virtually unaltered

and they were patronized by upper-class women as well as men. In George Williamson's words: 'the "proprietor" replaced the "host" in these establishments, serving the people who observed the proper proprieties in life.'

Alehouses were the original beer-drinking places: private houses that also played host to local people. During their long history they altered little, and country pubs today still owe much to their alehouse forebears, though most town pubs have changed out of all recognition.

The alehouse company would assemble in the living room, usually the kitchen, to drink the beer, which was stored in a room alongside it. Single-roomed pubs still exist on the original alehouse model, though most have had a best room or parlour added at some point, where those with aspirations to gentility could drink.

Alehouses existed everywhere and were the drinking place of those who were the forerunners of the industrial working class of the nineteenth century – farm labourers, small craftsmen and hired men. They were local people who used the alehouse solely as a place to drink and relax; it was not a place to trade or do business. There were many more alehouses than inns and taverns, and they became the prime customers for the brewers' products as commercial brewing began to replace the home-brewing once done by virtually all alehouses.

As this change took place, it was reflected in a parallel change in the town pub, from an alehouse to a more impersonal drink shop, and in the status of the landlord from independent owner or lessor to brewery tenant and then to manager. These changes in the roles of pubs and breweries mirrored the changes taking place throughout British manufacturing and retailing, as the old pre-industrial society of hand production and barter gave way to mass production and mass retailing.

The brewing industry was revolutionized just as much as textiles and engineering were by changes in technology and production methods. Improvements in the production of

A Taverner (Woodcut from Caxton's The Game of Chesse)

A Victorian pub interior of the 1880s

beer from the late eighteenth century onwards gave the commercial brewers an edge in price and quality over the home-brewers that they were quick to exploit. As the pubs ceased to home-brew, the commercial brewers tied them up with loans and acquired the freeholds of the many pubs that went bankrupt. By the mid-nineteenth century the brewers had sufficient capital either to build their own pubs or finance the emerging breed of speculative pub builders.

In the rural alehouses, as in the pre-nineteenth century shops, much trading went on by barter, a few eggs or a rabbit for a few pints of beer. The emergence of the formal pub and the formal retail shop put an end to this in the towns, shop assistants sold mass-produced goods at pre-determined prices and were not allowed to barter, and the pubs were the same. The rural areas continued in their old ways, but the town pubs were irrevocably changed. The alehouse of the peasants and artisans became the public house of the growing labour force who both produced and consumed the manufactures of the industrial revolution.

Gin Palaces

When we refer to 'gin palaces' we are not usually being strictly correct. We are talking about the glittering late-Victorian and Edwardian town pubs built by brewers and speculators at the height of the pub building boom. The true gin palaces pre-date these by fifty years and more.

Gin was only introduced to England by the

court of William of Orange in the late seventeenth century, but within fifty years there were 9,000 gin shops in London alone. The gin shop was quite literally a shop. There were no seats and no food; spirits, wine and beer were sold over a counter to take away or drink on the premises. The stand-up drink shops of Glasgow and other Scottish cities in the bad old pre-liberalization days of the 1960s were perhaps the last survivors of the species.

Despite much moralizing about its evil influence, gin became a hugely popular drink with the working classes, never more so than in the 1820s, when the duty on gin and other spirits was sharply cut. Free trade campaigning and the need to control smuggling, which was rife, saw the excise duty on spirits slashed by two-thirds. The results were immediate – the consumption of spirits in gin shops and in 'beer-ons' (drink shops where only beer could legally be consumed on the premises) illegally selling spirits doubled and criminal convictions quadrupled. This led to a great public outcry, and, under pressure from the emerging Temperance Movement and from the brewers, whose commercial interests were severely threatened, the Duke of Wellington's 1830 Beer Act was passed, allowing anyone to obtain a 'beer-on' licence for two guineas and removing excise duty from beer. Again, the results were unsurprising; 30,000 new 'beer-ons' were opened in the next twelve months and 50,000 in the next six years. To counter this assault on their commercial interests, the distillers began to open 'gin-palaces' to tempt their former customers back with lavish decor and fittings.

The Beer Act had obviously been rather too successful, and it was rescinded in 1869, a decision helped by the increasingly strong Temperance Movement. Many 'beer-ons' were closed down by the magistrates and many others were bought up by the brewers, who began installing tenants as a more direct way of controlling the trade. Previously they had been content with a tie on the products sold in return for paying the lease or the ground rent.

The attempts to impose temperance had an unexpected side-effect, however, as Mark Girouard points out in *Victorian Pubs*: 'One of the ironies of the Temperance Movement was that by successfully reducing the number of pubs and scaring the brewers into buying them in order to secure their markets, it helped to inflate the price of public house property. The buying, doing-up or rebuilding and selling of pubs became tempting speculations.' The 1890s were the peak of this speculative boom and many of the most lavish town pubs that still survive date from this time.

An early Victorian barmaid

As the expanding city populations were swollen by floods of new arrivals from the country, their pubs maintained, for a short while, many of the social functions of rural pubs. The general taste was not for rural-type pubs, though, but for brash city pubs, the brewery counterparts of the mid-century gin palaces. These town pubs were lavishly decorated, offering an escape from the often grim reality of the lives of many of their customers.

Like the cinemas of the 1930s, the nineteenth-century town pubs were places where people could relax in surroundings of considerable opulence, style and elegance, forgetting, for a short time, the relative poverty

An alehouse illustrated in a seventeenth-century pamphlet

and drabness of their home environment. For similar reasons there was also a great demand for entertainment, and more and more pubs used their upstairs rooms to put on shows. Music halls grew up as part of pubs, though by the turn of the century they had largely cut the ties and become separate institutions.

Brewers competed recklessly to build the most grandiose and lavish pubs, and the sums being invested by the 1890s far exceeded any possible returns. Pubs were changing hands for prices that were not reached again until the 1960s. The bubble had to burst, and when it did, millions of pounds of brewers' money was lost and many speculators were bankrupted. The story of one of the most spectacular crashes – Crocker's – is told later in the book. The disaster virtually put an end to the great pub-building era in the south, though in the north and midlands, where the brewers owned a higher percentage of pubs, it continued up to the First World War, by which time 95 per cent of pubs were tied houses

The Pub Interior

The change in town pubs from houses serving drink to drink shops, like the change from home to commercial brewing, was fuelled by technological advances. The introduction of a counter between the landlord and his customers was a direct result of the invention in the 1790s of the beer engine, which made possible the widespread use of cooler underground cellars. Prior to this, beer was usually kept in a ground floor store and brought through to customers by potmen and potboys, but the beer engine was installed in the room where the customers sat and, as glasses or tankards had to be stored alongside it, a barrier was needed to keep customers from helping themselves. So began the counter, servery and 'public' bar, though potboys still served in other rooms of the pub.

Before the development of the clear Burton ales, beer was a dark, murky liquid served in pewter or earthenware tankards. The lifting of the glass tax and improvements in the manufacture of bottles and glasses led to bottled and draught pale ales being drunk from clear glasses and these, too, had to be stored behind the bar. The position and size of the bar became all-important in the layout of the pub, with a central bar being the most efficient way of serving the multitude of small rooms that proliferated in Victorian pubs as a result of the other great force of change in nineteenth-century pubs – social pressure.

The development of a number of snugs, saloons, bars and parlours, smoke rooms, music rooms, ladies' bars and news rooms allowed a number of different groups with different requirements to be housed under one roof. The rigidities of the Victorian class system dictated that, for example, the petit bourgeois overlookers and clerks at a textile mill would wish to drink away from the eyes of the millhands. As all these groups lived within a close radius of their place of work, the private bars, snugs and snob screens, with their attendant higher prices, were the only way for these people to avoid the eyes of those who knew them. To lose face before a social inferior when the worse for drink was more than any good Victorian could contemplate.

The most obvious division, which, to some extent, has continued to the present day, is that between the blue-collar public bar and the white-collar saloon, though the erosion of class barriers and the affluence of post Second World War Britain has persuaded many breweries to demolish partitions and charge all customers the higher saloon bar prices.

Improvements in public transport and, more particularly, the development of the motor car, later enabled people to live farther from their place of work. As they had the means and the leisure time to travel more widely, there was less need for those who wanted to drink unobserved to seek a physical separation from other pub customers. They would be unknown and un-recognized without having to hide behind snob screens.

Among other changes that gave rise to the typical look of Victorian pubs was the increase in literacy which allowed brewers to advertise their wares on the exteriors and interiors of their pubs. The invention of plate glass and the development of engraving, etching, brilliant cutting, embossing and silvering allowed small-panes to be replaced with the characteristic large windows, bearing the brewery name. Gas lighting was available for the first time. The counter and backfitting were located in the public part of the pub. The pub as a shop had arrived and would reign unchallenged for as long as Queen Victoria herself.

The Temperance Movement

Pubs had a fairly disreputable image around the turn of the century – only elegant 'slummers' of the upper classes would patronize them – and up to the outbreak of the First World War, the pub was under sustained attack. An increasingly strong, confident and vociferous temperance lobby was joined in its attacks by those who saw drink as a prime cause of the industrial and social unrest sweeping through the industrialized world.

The rise of the Temperance Movement saw an end to many of the functions once performed by pubs. Tax collectors and coroners no longer

The Edinburgh Castle in Limehouse was the Temperance Movement's answer to the gin palace – a 'coffee palace'. The number of customers shown was probably an exaggeration!

used them and election meetings were no longer held in them, for both the Liberal and Labour parties had strong temperance elements within their ranks. Despite this, they remained and still remain, home to the myriad arcane societies and groupings in which the British involve themselves at play. Everything from trainspotters, pigeon-fanciers and leek-growers to the Royal and Antediluvian Order of Buffaloes meets in pubs.

The temperance lobby within the Liberals was further strengthened by Lloyd George's leadership of the Party. A teetotaller, Lloyd George was responsible for the one piece of parliamentary legislation that has created more anger than any other – the licensing laws. Until the First World War, pubs were open all day. Lloyd George's 'temporary measure', introduced with the aim of helping the War Effort by improving the sobriety of troops and munitions workers, has remained in force ever since, to the considerable annoyance of both British citizens and foreign visitors.

State control of pubs and breweries was also introduced at this time in key areas, notably around Carlisle and Gretna with its massive munitions factories, where the State Management Scheme, as it was known, first came into operation. Many pubs were closed down and new ones constructed where the aim was to create strong counter-attractions to the 'demon drink'. Newspapers were provided and games were encouraged, with most pubs having bowling greens and snooker tables, and drunkenness was forbidden. No customers showing signs of intoxication nor people of 'loose morals' were to be served, 'treating' (the buying of rounds) was forbidden, and minimal advertising of drink was permitted.

The scheme, like all other attempts at compulsory abstinence, was a failure. Far from reducing consumption, the curtailment of licensing hours serves only to increase the quantity and tempo of drinking. The 'six o'clock swill' in Australia, the 'ten o'clock swill' in pre-liberalization Glasgow, prohibition in the United States and the State Management Scheme in Carlisle all point to the same conclusion.

The effects in Carlisle were absolutely predictable. Munitions workers coming off the evening shift in Gretna, would board the train to Carlisle and hold a whip-round for the driver, payable if he got them in ahead of schedule. All the pubs near the station would have beer and whisky lined up from one end of the bar to the other. When the train got to the station, a tidal wave of munitions workers would flood out into the pubs, down the lot in the twenty minutes or so available to them and then fall out

Pubs are often home to collections ranging from the unusual to the preposterous. This collection of foreign banknotes is in the Ship Inn at Shaftesbury

into the streets for a drunken rampage through the town, brawling, throwing up in the gutters, harassing the residents, molesting the towns-women and generally making the people of Car-lisle feel that a German invasion could scarcely be more unpleasant.

Despite this unpromising start, the Carlisle and District State Management Scheme lasted for almost sixty years, long after the First World War had ended, before being summarily dis-posed of by the Conservative government of the early 1970s, at a time when it had won the respect and affection of its customers even though trading under almost insuperable hand-icaps. A brewing and pub-owning company that

Elynour Rummynge, a sixteenth century 'ale wife', whose ale was almost certainly less intimidating than her features

is required to discourage drinking is at a major commercial disadvantage when trying to com-pete against companies with no such restric-tions to hamper them!

The Carlisle Scheme became the model for the movement for reformed and improved pubs which occurred in the 1920s and 1930s. Pub styles of the past were brought back, usually bearing remarkably little relation to the original. The most obvious style was 'Brewers' Tudor': hundreds of roadhouses clad in ersatz half-timbering sprouted throughout Britain and par-ticularly in the South, catering for the new car trade. Their bowling greens and tennis courts, and their emphasis on food and clean whole-some fun, created an atmosphere of tearoom gentility rather than public bar camaraderie. Drinking was regarded as at best peripheral to their function and in the case of the State Man-agement Scheme, something to be actively dis-couraged. These inter-war estate and roadside pubs have been generally unloved and their pas-sing provokes no great outcry; they were bogus creations separate from authentic public house traditions and inspire little of the affection that we feel for our traditional pubs.

The post-war period saw the beginnings of a move away from 'Brewers' Tudor', but a wave of brewery mergers in the 1960s was accompanied by a fresh flood of pub alterations. The new brewery giants replaced individual signing and decoration with their own liveries, and regarded pubs as simply retail outlets for beer. Changing social patterns, the increase in pub catering, the brewers' desire for higher prices and profits, and the police and magistrates' insistence on supervision from the bar of every part of the pub, led to the wholesale destruction of internal walls and partitions and the frequent disappearance of the public bar. From being havens for every section of the community, many town pubs became ghettoes for just one sector or age group.

Currently, the increasing use of pubs by women and families is having many beneficial effects. Relaxation of the licensing laws will also tend to make our pubs more civilized places. Sadly, though, in too many alterations and new developments, pub owners, architects and designers have lost sight of the values and traditions that make our pubs unique.

The opening-out of pub interiors creates problems by subjecting all the pub company to the often noisy pleasures of one particular group of customers. Pubs with separate rooms or, at least, separate drinking areas, can cope with families, food, juke boxes, smokers and a host of different groups without alienating pub-goers who do not share their tastes.

Even worse than the loss of separate rooms has been the attempt by several large companies to impose an identikit series of 'visions' upon our pubs. One of the greatest strengths of the pub is its individuality: for a company to deliberately create scores of identical 'theme pubs' in all parts of the country is both grotesque and short-sighted. Many of the results of the Victorian pub building and renovating boom have survived to the present day; those that have not have usually been lost to redevelopment of their communities. Today's 'theme' and 'fun' pubs are unlikely to last five years before another refit is ordered, at the customer's ultimate expense.

For the moment, much of our rich heritage of fine town and city pubs survives for us all to enjoy. They have witnessed great moments in our history and have also given more simple pleasure to more people than anything up to and including sliced bread. Here are one hundred classic town pubs, which make the arriving as much of a pleasure as the travelling. May you enjoy them all as much as I did, and may you be even luckier and find the ones that no-one else knows about as well!

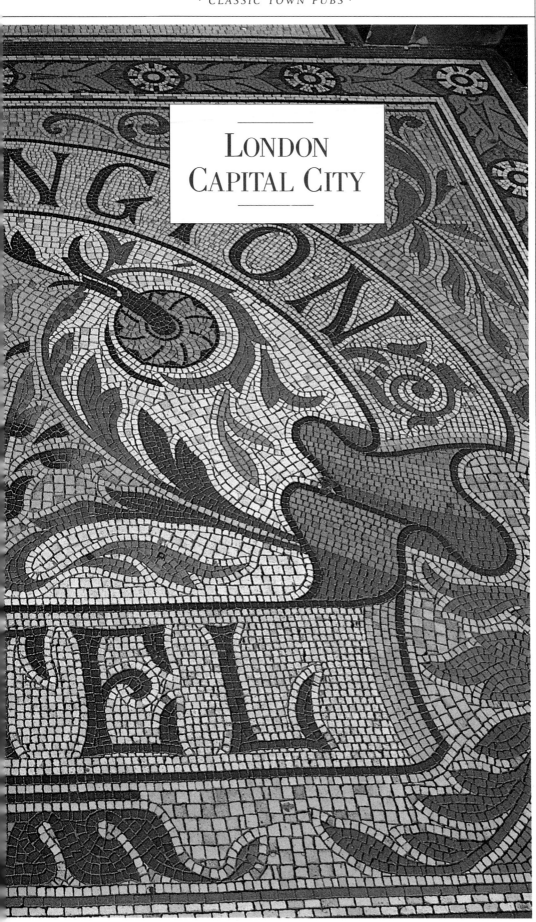

LONDON
CAPITAL CITY

London had been a major Celtic settlement for centuries before the Emperor Claudius founded the military camp of Londinium. The Romans fortified an area of about one square mile, which coincides roughly with the boundaries of the square mile of the City of London today. After briefly being captured by Boudicca (aka Boadicea) during the rebellion of 61 AD, London became an important port and the capital of one of the four Roman provinces of Britain.

The Roman withdrawal left London to be settled by waves of Angles, Saxons and Jutes and laid waste by hordes of Danes and Norsemen, but Alfred the Great, who took London in 886, began a period of growth, consolidated by Canute and Edward the Confessor, who both made Westminster their residence. William the Conqueror was crowned in Westminster Abbey, and built the White Tower at the Tower of London, though London did not replace Winchester as the English capital until the reign of Henry I in the twelfth century.

From then on, London developed as the principal trading city in England, with a population that rose to half a million by the sixteenth century. The Plague slashed the population by 70,000 in 1665, and the Great Fire of London destroyed three-quarters of the city the following year. Yet that catastrophe merely spurred London to a great rebuilding programme in which Christopher Wren was the dominant architect. London grew to be the heart of the Victorian Empire and has remained by far our largest and most important city to this day, surviving the destruction brought about by the Battle of Britain and at least some of that wrought by property developers.

Much of the pleasure of London comes from unexpected things: buildings and places that you find by accident. Don't be afraid to get lost; take an 'A to Z' or similar street plan and wander where the mood takes you. If your taste, like mine, tends to the quirky and bizarre, the capital is a treasure house. Keep your eyes open, especially above ground floor level, and you will quickly make your own discoveries.

My favourite is probably the 'Decency Forbids – Lavatory Opposite' sign in a dark alley off Bayswater Road, inviting Victorian gentlemen to please refrain! There is the Cherry Pie Memorial on the George Inn, Wanstead, carved by two builders who were fined in 1752 for stealing a cherry pie from the tray of a passing pieman: 'In Memory of ye Cherry Pye As cost 1/2 a Guiney ye 17 of July. That day we had good cheer Hope to do so many a year.'

The disgusting bun collection in The Widow's Son pub in Devons Road, Bow, is also worth a look. An eighteenth-century widow baked a hot cross bun every Easter for her sailor son, away at sea. Until she died, she baked and kept her annual hot cross buns in the hope that he would one day return home. He never did. The pub built on the site of her cottage has maintained the tradition, and every Good Friday, a sailor adds another bun to the mummified collection hanging over the bar.

In a lane in the City stands the golden boy of Cock Lane, a gilded statue which used to have an inscription recording that it was erected in memory of the Fire of London. 'occasioned by the sin of gluttony', an abstruse reference to the fact that the fire started in Pudding Lane and was finally extinguished on the site of the statue at Pie Corner. Another splendid statue, of William III, stands in St James Square, featuring the molehill that was responsible for his death by tripping his horse. His opponents commemorated the occasion with great relish in toasts to 'the little gentleman in velvet'.

Above Carter's shop in the Old Kent Road is the figure of a man who raises his bowler hat every day at noon. In Borough High Street (near the George, which we shall shortly be visiting) stands a church with four clock faces. Three of these are illuminated at night, but the fourth faces Bermondsey, whose parishioners would not contribute to an appeal for funds, and as a punishment that face is black and unlit at night!

A bust of Shakespeare leaning out of a window above the Shakespeare's Head pub, is a surprising addition to Carnaby Street, and in Carting Lane in the Strand, there is a gas lamp which had a surprising source of illumination. With typical Victorian resourcefulness, these lamps were designed to burn on the appalling stench of methane piped up from the sewers below! Last, and quite possibly least, Euston Station – you have to laugh or you'd cry!

So much for the potted history and curios; now for a look at some of London's magnificent collection of classic pubs!

The George Inn is one of London's most magnificent pubs and yet it hides shyly down an alleyway off the A3, once a vital coaching route to the ports of the south coast. That same route also brought hops from Kent to the capital with the result that the borough of Southwark became a vital and vibrant brewing area of London, based around the Hop Exchange, a vast and ornate building now being restored to its former grandeur. Courage, Barclay Perkins and Thrale all had breweries in Southwark and Dr Samuel Johnson, a regular visitor to the George before dining with the Thrales, was profitably involved in the sale of

The galleried George at Southwark, an historic pub in the Shakespearian tradition

his friends' Anchor Brewery to Barclay Perkins.

Southwark was an area of entertainment as well as boozing. Shakespeare's Globe Theatre was close by and it is reputed that his strolling players performed in the courtyard and from the galleries of the George. The original inn was destroyed in the Great Fire of 1666, which also ravaged most of Southwark (the spot where the fire broke out in Pudding Lane is marked by the Monument on the other side of London Bridge). The inn was rebuilt in 1677 and is the last surviving Elizabethan galleried inn in London. It once occupied three sides of the courtyard but when its owners, the trustees of Guy's Hospital, sold it to the London and North Eastern Railway Company in the nineteenth century, the railway barons thoughtlessly reduced the inn in order to use some of the buildings as engine sheds. They have long gone but the inn, its presence marked by a sign in Borough High Street, remains in galleried and beamed glory.

The ground floor bars of the George are small and low-ceilinged, with lattice windows, bare-boarded floors and wooden settles. The back bar, nearest to the main road, has a Parliamentary clock, commemorating the time when Parliament, in one of its mad moods, imposed a tax on timepieces. The serving area through a hatch has a fine example of a Victorian 'cash register' beer engine. A corridor leads to a long, narrow, central bar and then into a more spacious room used for eating. Upstairs, elegant rooms are set aside for more serious dining.

A visit to the George is a memorable occasion, recalling the heady times of the first Elizabeth. The pub is owned by the National Trust, but it is a living pub, not a quaint museum piece.

If and when you tire of the George, cross Borough High Street and thread your way through the busy streets of the vegetable market that surrounds the splendour of Southwark Cathedral and down to the Thames. Keep to your left through the maze of small streets and warehouses, which are finding new life as offices and restaurants, under Southwark Bridge, and you come to Bankside and the awesome bulk of the Bankside power station. In its shadow on the embankment is the antithesis of the George, the ultra modern Founders Arms.

When Young & Co, the fervently traditional independent brewers in Wandsworth, were given the contract to build the Founders Arms, they mercifully avoided the temptation to create some fake-and-flummery 'olde worlde' tourist haunt. The Founders is modern and sensible, offering superb views of the Thames from a wall composed

The George Inn
Licensees: J.E. Hall & C.R.F. Symes
77 Borough High Street, London SE1
☎ (01) 407 2056
11 - 3; 5.30 - 11

Brakspear Bitter; Green King Abbot; Flowers Original; Wethereds Bitter

Lunchtime & evening food. Separate dining-rooms on first floor. Courtyard drinking area.

London Bridge Station (British Rail and Northern Line)

The Founders Arms, a fine pub with possibly the best view in London

entirely of glass. An earlier pub on the site bore the same name and marked the spot where foundries forged the bells for Christopher Wren's St Paul's Cathedral across the river. Wren lived nearby and watched his great creation refashioning the Thameside skyline. It is an inspiring sight to sit in the Founders or on its terrace on a warm evening as the sun goes down and the spotlights pick out both St Paul's and the spire of St Bride's in Fleet Street, which in turn cast their shadows across the river.

The pub has ample banquette seating, and pillars that divide the long room into cheerful segments, all served by a long bar pumping out pints of Young's exceptionally tasty and tangy bitters. A raised area at the end closest to Blackfriars Bridge is set aside as a separate dining area. On my visit the licensee expressed considerable surprise at his inclusion in the guide: 'This is not a classic,' he said. 'It's too new.' But the Founders proves that it is possible to be both new and superb.

The Founders is just a few minutes' walk from arguably the most astonishing pub creation in London. Go along Hopton Street, climb the steps up to Blackfriars Bridge and cross the Thames. At the junction of Queen Victoria Street and New Bridge Street stands the remarkable, wedge-shaped Black Friar.

The Black Friar is one of the finest examples of art-nouveau architecture in London. The pub was built in 1903, designed by H. Fuller Clarke with designs by the sculptor Henry Poole. It was a sensation, a bibu-

The marbled halls of London's Black Friar, saved from the threat of demolition to delight lovers of art nouveau and great pubs alike

Founders Arms
Licensees: C.P.W. Read & D.A. Irvin-Turner
Hopton Street,
(off Southwark Street),
London SE1
☎ (01) 928 1899/1890
11 - 3; 5.30 - 11

Youngs Bitter; Special Bitter

Bar food Monday to Friday, Restaurant (closed Saturday lunchtime & Sunday evening). Children allowed in restaurant. Terraced drinking area.

Blackfriars Station (British Rail and District and Circle Lines)

Black Friar
Licensee: David McKinstry
174 Queen Victoria Street,
London EC4
☎ (01) 236 5650
11 - 3; 5.30 - 11 (closed Saturday evening and all day Sunday).

Adnams Bitter; Boddingtons Bitter; Draught Bass; Tetley Bitter

Lunchtime food (not Saturday).

Blackfriars Station (British Rail and District and Circle Lines)

The exterior of the Black Friar – with a pub as good as this, no wonder the friars are jolly!

lous shrine to a Dominican priory that once stood on the site. The bronze and marble exterior has panels showing friars urgently pointing to the interior. A frieze of panels inside extends the theme, with the jocular friars, fishing, singing and sleeping off their carousing. Tongue-in-cheek engraved slogans tell customers that 'Silence is Golden', 'Wisdom is Rare' and 'Industry is All'. 'A Good Thing is Soon Snatched Up' is clearly a reference to the wide range of excellent draught beers served from the marble bar. Marble abounds, from walls and pillars to the inglenook fireplace. The elegant back room has vast mirrors set into the marble walls.

Nicholsons, a division of Allied Breweries, have spent close on a million pounds lovingly restoring the Black Friar and sensibly running it as a free house. Fruit machines have been removed (what would the friars have thought?) and the front bar, the sharp end of the wedge, offers excellent home-prepared lunchtime meals and snacks at reasonable prices.

The pub attracts great crowds, not just tourists, but office workers and journalists from what is left of the Fleet Street newspaper industry. When the weather is kind, drinkers spill out on to the small pedestrian area that marks the end of New Bridge Street.

The best time to visit the Black Friar is before the lunch and evening hordes descend. In its quieter moments you can enjoy to the full this unique memorial to the ecclesiastically approved pleasures of drinking!

There are several other excellent riverside pubs in London, including the Mayflower at Rotherhithe, from where the Pilgrim Fathers set sail for America, but while you are at Blackfriars, nip into the station and take a train to Denmark Hill, where you will find a boisterous boozer in great contrast to the Black Friar's marbled halls.

As the name suggests, the Phoenix & Firkin arose from the ashes of the old Denmark Hill Station, gutted by fire in 1980. British Rail decided that the old station hall was too large for their needs, and David Bruce stepped in to convert it to another of his highly successful chain of 'Firkin' pubs. The formula is simple: stripped wood, old brick, beer brewed on the premises and a robust and lively atmosphere. In fact, it's the 'back to basics' movement, of which Bruce is the founding father.

There are Firkins all over London, but the Phoenix is possibly the best, certainly the most characterful. The echoing station hall has been converted into a large, high-ceilinged bar, complete with a huge station clock, rescued from a station in Wales. Seating is at church pews and

The Phoenix & Firkin
Licensees: Mr & Mrs S.A. Smith
5 Windsor Walk,
Denmark Hill,
London SE5
☎ (01) 701 8282
11 - 3; 5.30 - 11

Bruce's Brewery Rail, Phoenix, Dogbolter; Guest beers

Lunchtime & evening food. Families welcome.

Denmark Hill Station (British Rail)

rough wooden tables, while a spiral staircase leads up to a balconied loft, offering a fine view of any bald patches on the heads of customers below.

Through a double arch from the main bar is another bar and food servery, offering pies, salads, cold cuts and a hot dish of the day – food for hungry drinkers rather than cuisine nouvelle. Outside is an area where you can sit at genuine British Rail benches beneath a wrought iron canopy. The pub is quietest at lunchtime, heaving at night, and brash and gutsy like all Bruce's pubs; a good place for a lively night out. CAMRA purists avoid the home-brewed beer, which is kept under a light carbon dioxide

Phoenix from the ashes – the Phoenix & Firkin, resurrected from the 'ashes' of Denmark Hill Station

blanket, but the guest beers are guaranteed free of extraneous gas.

Take the train back to Blackfriars Station, then walk up New Bridge Street to Ludgate Circus. On the right is a fine view of St Paul's. To the left is Fleet Street, with a clutch of pubs catering for the declining number of journalists and print workers there.

A sign in Fleet Street lures you up the alley where you will find Ye Olde Cheshire Cheese, and despite its worldwide fame, the Cheese retains the character and atmosphere that makes it a must for any pub-lover in London. A maze of smoke-blackened, sawdust-strewn rooms meander around three floors of this ancient building, rebuilt in 1667 after the original inn was destroyed in the Great Fire of London.

The Cheese is one of the few Chop Houses –

Ye Olde Cheshire Cheese – perhaps the most famous pub in the world, certainly one of the finest

Ye Olde Cheshire Cheese
Licensee: Gordon Garrity
Wine Office Court,
145 Fleet Street,
London EC4
☎ (01) 353 6170/4388
11.30 - 3; 5 - 9. Closed
Saturday & Sunday

Samuel Smith Old Brewery
Bitter, Museum Ale

Lunchtime & evening food.
Families welcome.

Holborn Viaduct or Black-
friars Stations (British Rail
and District and Circle
Lines)

the seventeenth-century forerunners of the steak house – still surviving. Dr Johnson and Charles Dickens, who are among its many famous past customers, would notice little change in the pub interior from their own eras. Off the central corridor is a bar, until quite recently men-only, with a large fireplace. Its panelling and beams are blackened with age and smoke. Opposite is the Chop Room, where you can sit at wooden benches and eat, not chops, but the Cheese's justly famous steak, kidney and mushroom or game pies and puddings, or their excellent roast beef.

Upstairs are two more bars, one for eating and one for drinking, while at the back of the pub, the windows of the Cheese face onto a small area with a sloping flagstone floor, once an alley behind the pub, now a part of it. Down a perilous set of stairs is the cellar bar, with oak beams and uneven flagstones, worn by centuries of use. There are plenty of equally ancient pubs that have been ruined by 'improvement' schemes; the Cheshire Cheese is one that has remained untouched and unspoilt, perhaps *the* London pub.

Stroll back down across Ludgate Circus and Old Bailey looms on your left; in its shadow is the next London classic pub.

The leaded windows of the narrow frontage of the Magpie & Stump look directly onto the Old Bailey, and the pub's connection with some of the more, and less, savoury aspects of law and order go back over 250 years. Before the Old Bailey was built, the site was occupied by the infamous Newgate Gaol. 'We shall never forget the mingled feelings of awe and respect with which we looked on the exterior of Newgate in our schooldays,' wrote Charles Dickens, and he uses Newgate scenes in *Sketches by Boz, Barnaby Rudge, Oliver Twist* and *Great Expectations*. Dickens even attended two public executions there, as part of his campaign for their abolition; many others attended them just for the free 'entertainment'.

During the eighteenth and nineteenth centuries the landlords of the Magpie & Stump used to augment their income by renting out the top floors of the pub to upper-class revellers, who would stage all-night parties there on the night before an execution, watch the hanging at dawn and then consume an 'execution breakfast' before returning home to bed. A copy of the Reverend Richard Harris Barham's contemporary satirical poem about such an event, hangs on the wall of the narrow front bar. You can still capture a little of the mood on Sunday lunchtimes, when 'execution breakfasts' are served.

Perhaps that is just as well, for it was a particularly hideous spectacle, only abolished in 1868. The victim stood under the gallows on a cart, the rope was put around his neck and the cart was then driven off, leaving the hapless victim dangling, to suffer death by a very slow strangulation. Friends of the victim would often add their weight to his legs, to try and bring the merciful end a little nearer.

The Magpie & Stump (which may have acquired the second half of its name from the grisly remnants of the public executions) is regularly used by the barristers and journalists who follow their trades in the most famous criminal court in the world, and also by Post Office workers, giving it a surprisingly local atmosphere for a pub in the heart of the City. As proof of this, it boasts a string of quiz league teams and is one of the few pubs in the City that stays open until the normal pub-closing time; most shut their doors in mid-evening, when the last of the city gents has gone home.

There is a narrow beamed and panelled bar at the front with a food servery. At the back is an atmospheric saloon with pictures of old London, all with some connection with the pub, on the panelled walls. There are plaster reliefs of magpies behind the bar, a motif repeated in the upstairs bar, which also has a fine ceiling. The decor dates from 1931, when the pub was last remodelled. At lunchtime the upstairs bar serves as a dining room, in the evening it is used for functions.

The Magpie & Stump has its share of macabre past associations, but they are unlikely to spoil your appetite for the 'execution break-

The Magpie & Stump
Licensee: Gregory Charters
18 Old Bailey,
London EC4
11.30 - 3; 5 - 11. Closed Saturday evening.

Draught Bass; Charrington IPA; Young Bitter

Lunchtime & evening food. Families welcome. Restaurant.

Holborn Viaduct Station (British Rail) or St Paul's (Central Line)

The Magpie & Stump has looked out on sights that would shock even the most hardened habitués of the Old Bailey

fast' or for the excellent bread which is baked at the pub every day. The pub is living proof that all the warmth and atmosphere of a small town local can be found even in the heart of the City.

The Old Mitre – the jewel of Hatton Garden

At the top of Old Bailey turn left and cross over the Holborn Viaduct into Holborn Circus. To the north is Hatton Garden, the world-famous centre of the jewellery business, where another remarkable pub awaits us. The shops offer a great choice of jewels and watches but it is best to avert your gaze unless you have a special relationship with your bank. Keep your eyes open, however, for an old-fashioned street lamp on the right which marks the entrance to Ely Court.

The Olde Mitre, tucked away down a courtyard that leads into the elegant Ely Place, has a fascinating history. It is a careful replica of a tavern built in 1546 for the servants of the Bishops of Ely who held sway over the area. The bishops' diocese was Ely in Cambridgeshire and for centuries the pub was licensed not in London but by the Cambridge magistrates. Although the rule is not enforced, the City of London police should get permission from the licensing bench to enter the premises.

Ely Place was the centre of religious and political power. John of Gaunt's 'This sceptr'd isle' speech in Shakespeare's *Richard II* was made there. In 1576 the bishops' power was diluted when Sir Christopher Hatton took control of Ely Place. A preserved cherry tree (around which Good Queen Bess is alleged to have danced) in the environs of the Mitre marks the boundary between the land leased to Hatton and the bishops' garden. During the English Civil War the tavern was used as both a prison and a hospital.

The present pub has a small front bar and a larger back one, with beams, old settles and oak-panelled walls. The two bars are linked by a central serving area. At busy times, drinkers spill out of the bars into the tiny area, with a few seats, between the pub and St Ethelreda's church, itself an interesting historical curio. It is the only London church that has reverted to Catholicism since the Reformation.

Now take a wander back past St Paul's and through the heart of the City of London. Pass the doors of the Bank of England itself and make your way to Leadenhall, where another excellent pub, the Lamb Tavern, awaits you.

The Lamb stands right beside the magnificent entrance to Leadenhall market, with its huge iron pillars topped by snarling iron dragons. The market is Victorian but is now sandwiched between several late-

Olde Mitre
Licensee: Michael Kennedy
Ely Court,
off Ely Place,
London EC1
☎ (01) 405 4751
11 - 3; 5.30 - 11. Closed weekends

Friary Meux Bitter; Ind Coope Burton Ale; Tetley Bitter

Snacks lunchtime and evening.

Chancery Lane Station (Central Line)

twentieth century temples to Mammon – the new Lloyds building and the Legal and General building to name but two. Despite its market location, the Lamb's trade is very definitely the city gents and serious money brigade; on my last visit, one Thursday lunchtime, with the pub packed to the rafters on all four floors and spilling out into the market, I was the only male customer not wearing a city suit. The Lamb was built in 1780 and is a Grade II listed building. The market it serves was rebuilt in 1881, though the sort of market traders the pub attracts now do their trading on telephones and VDUs, rather than stalls and barrows.

In the basement are the Wine Bar and Smok-

The Lamb Tavern, Leadenhall – a Victorian oasis in the concrete canyons of the City

ing Room, a series of interlinked rooms with tiled walls, served from a curved bar. A darts area has two boards, both in constant use. The main entrance has a fine tiled mural and there is a large bar with a spiral staircase leading to a mezzanine area. A separate flight of stairs leads up to the City of London's first and, at the time of writing, the only no-smoking bar, a light and airy room which also has a food servery. Around the walls are portraits of some of the Young Brewery directors in Victorian times.

As a dedicated tourist you will, of course, wish to spend the obligatory half hour in Oxford Street. The Argyll, near Oxford Circus makes a good retreat, but the next classic pub is to be found in the tranquillity of Bloomsbury, where you should head with all speed.

The Lamb Tavern
Licensee: David Morris
10-12 Leadenhall Market, London EC3
☎ (01) 626 2454
11.30 - 3; 5 - 9.30. Closed Saturday evenings and all day Sunday.

Youngs Bitter, Special, Winter Warmer

Lunchtime food. No-smoking bar.

Bank Station (Northern and Central Lines)

Snobscreens in the Lamb, Lamb's Conduit Street – discretion assured, satisfaction guaranteed!

Literary London is focused on Bloomsbury; publishers, bookshops, the British Museum and British Library. Literature can be dry and dusty stuff, however, and a break in the Lamb in Lambs Conduit Street may provide a welcome relief.

The Lamb has fine, etched glass windows and a handsome façade looking out onto Lamb's Conduit Street. The interior is warmly welcoming, always lively, and notable for the magnificent, etched and brilliant cut snob screens, which completely ring the central bar. Open them for eyeball-to-eyeball contact with the bar staff or close them and watch as a disembodied hand collects your money and delivers your drink.

Around the side of the room are some of the most comfortable old leather seats you will ever sink into; on the walls above them are hundreds of sepia pictures of Victorian music hall stars. Down a couple of steps beyond the food counter there are more seats, and outside is a small drinking area, though in fine weather you are as likely to find people spilling out into Lamb's Conduit Street at the front.

What makes the Lamb so pleasant is that it is a truly delightful and absolutely genuine pub. Its custom is a remarkably wide mixture, all enjoying the superb Young's beer and indulging in that most pleasant and underrated of pub pursuits, conversation. There is no canned muzak and no gimmicks, it is not a yuppie brasserie or a restaurant – it is simply a pub, and one of the best in London

The Lamb
Licensees: Richard & Rosemary Whyte
94 Lamb's Conduit Street, London WC1
☎ (01) 405 0713
11 - 3; 5.30 - 11

Young Bitter, Special, Winter Warmer

Lunchtime & evening food. Small outside drinking area.

Russell Square Station (Piccadilly Line)

Opposite: The unique interior of 'Crocker's Folly'

So much for literature, now for sport! If you have been paying homage at the temple of cricket, Lords, and you are in the mood for a bite to eat, a bewildering range of beers and the most magnificent pub you will ever come across, you are in luck. Leave the crowds trying to elbow their way into the Lords Tavern and wander along St Johns Wood Road to Cunningham Place, which will lead you to Aberdeen Place and Crockers.

The medieval monk who spent fifty years producing a magnificent illumination of the title page of the gospel according to St Mattew or the fire insurance salesman who started work in London in 1666, would have had a lot of sympathy for Frank Crocker. Mr Crocker was a shrewd Victorian who realized that the building of the great London railway stations provided the chance of a bonanza for those smart enough to have built hotels just across the road from them. Acting on information received, Mr Crocker scooped his fellow entrepreneurs, siting a magnificent hotel right across the road from the soon-to-be-built Marylebone Station. He sat back, rubbing his hands in glee as the line approached closer and closer to Aberdeen Place.

Gradually, however, his glee turned to glumness as the line continued smoothly past, disappearing a country mile further in towards London, to the present site of Marylebone Station. The distraught Mr Crocker was ruined, with no customers to fill the bars and bedrooms of The Crown (as it was then called). He threw himself to his death from the roof of Crocker's Folly, as his callous locals re-named it, leaving as his monument the finest late-Victorian pub in London . . . and certainly the most magnificent station hotel in the world that doesn't have a station anywhere near it!

The Crown was in a sad state of disrepair when it was purchased by its present owners, Vaux Breweries, in 1983, and they deserve praise for the way they have restored it to close to its original condition. At the same time, they changed its name to commemorate its creator.

The frontage of Crockers gives you some idea of what to expect when you step inside – but only some. The bar just might take your breath away. It has the most ornate ceiling I have ever seen in a pub, all purple and gold, about a dozen kinds of marble and a unique fireplace. There is a food servery at the far end of the main bar and mahogany doors lead through to the Music Room. This has a different but equally elaborate ceiling, another remarkable marble fireplace and a stage at one end, from where you will be offered live entertainment at least a couple of nights per week. In any other pub the public bar would seem elaborate, but

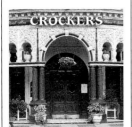

Crocker's – the road to bankruptcy is paved with railway sleepers!

Crockers
Licensee: Peter Cox
Aberdeen Place,
Maida Vale,
London NW8
☎ (01) 286 6608
11 - 3; 5.30 (6 Saturday) - 11

Darley Thorne Best Bitter; Vaux Samson; Ward Sheffield Best Bitter; Several guest beers

Lunchtime & evening food. Families welcome in Music Room.

Warwick Avenue Station (Bakerloo Line)

here its gilt cherubs seem rather down-market by comparison with the grandeur of the main bar!

Frank Crocker's ghost is said to wander the building still, no doubt reflecting that if the pub had been half as busy when he was alive, he wouldn't have had to throw himself off the roof.

Maida Vale is certainly the place to be for Victorian curiosities, for just across the other side of the main road is the Warrington Hotel, another magnificent Victorian pub and one which I am pretty confident in saying has a unique pedigree. It is surely the only pub in Britain that was once a brothel owned by the Church of England!

The main entrance is beautiful, its pillars and facia covered in superb art-nouveau tiling, its mosaic floors flanked by fine, wrought-iron lamps. Inside is a vast, curved, marble-topped bar. There are marble pillars, a fine fireplace and some ever-so-slightly risqué murals on the canopy over the bar and around the walls.

On a shelf above the fireplace of the main bar is an empty champagne bottle, the last bottle that the great music hall star Marie Lloyd drank in the Warrington (there had been quite a few before that one). Both Marie Lloyd and her champagne are long gone, but the bottle and the memory linger on. The taproom, like that at Crockers, is spartan only in contrast to the splendours of the main bar. There is a fine, wood and cast-iron fireplace, etched glass and another ornate ceiling.

Risqué murals are also a feature of the function room upstairs, which no doubt saw sights that would have caused a blush or two in the downstairs bar, and something close to apoplexy in those members of the Church of England not aware of the more unorthodox uses for church property!

Either Crockers or the Warrington makes an excellent departure point for the north and north-west. Just head up the A5 and you can be on the M1 in no time or in St Albans before you can say Watling Street. Before you leave London behind there are another two very different, but equally excellent, north London pubs which will not take you too far off your route.

Hampstead and Highgate mark the northern frontiers of old London, once the elegant resting places of the haute bourgeoisie, with a writers' and artists' enclave, now leafy residential homes for better-heeled city workers, with easy access to the A1 and M1. From the open spaces of Hampstead Heath and Parliament Hill you can look over the great sprawl of the city, as far as the Crystal Palace

The Warrington Hotel
Licensees: David Williams & John Brandon
93 Warrington Crescent, London W9
11 - 3; 5.30 - 11

Arkell BB; Brakspear Special Bitter; Fuller London Pride, ESB; Young Special

Lunchtime food. Outside drinking area. Function room.

Warwick Avenue or Maida Vale Station (Bakerloo Line)

The Warrington Hotel – the stairway to heaven in the Church of England's brothel!

The Holly Bush, a sure source of 'appiness in 'Ampstead!

aerial on a clear day. Noble houses nestle with bookshops, galleries and smart eating places. The two villages, as they are always called, are linked by Spaniards Way with Kenwood House and grounds, where fine pictures and open-air classical concerts can be enjoyed.

The Holly Bush is a trip back to Victorian and Edwardian London. A faint, illusory mist seems to hang around the lamp-lit exterior in the evening. From the Underground station, walk up Heath Street for a hundred yards or so and as soon as you pass the Nag's Head pub on the left get ready for the short but sharp climb up the steps to Holly Mount, where you will find the picturesque pub on a bend to the right. The rambling warren of a building dates back to well before the time of Queen Victoria. It was formerly the home of the painter George Romney who died in 1802 and what is now the back bar was once his stables. On his death, the building was sold to the Hampstead Constitutional Club, who then sold it to a local licensed victualler. He in turn sold out to Benskins, the Watford brewery, who found a rare North London outlet for their ales.

The gas-lit front bar and rooms have a fund of Benskins artefacts on the panelled walls. The area is divided by half-glazed partitions into several smaller, snug areas. A narrow passage leads into the George Romney room, less successfully refurbished with ochre-painted brickwork, though there is a fine Ind Coope mirror. The joy of this unspoilt old pub is that, even at its busiest, there are always quiet corners where you can enjoy your ale and conversation in an atmosphere that recalls a time when the village was 'Appy 'Ampstead and artisans rubbed shoulders with rising entrepreneurs, artists and writers

The Holly Bush
Licensees: Peter Dures & Nicholas Leach
Holly Mount,
off Heath Street,
London NW3
11 - 3; 5.30 - 11

Benskins Bitter; Ind Coope Burton Ale; Tetley Bitter

Lunchtime food. Evening food Tuesday to Saturday.

Hampstead Station (Northern Line)

Brewery memorabilia in the Holly Bush

The Flask is a low-slung sprawl of a pub, first built in 1663 and rebuilt in 1767. The highwayman Dick Turpin escaped his pursuers here and such luminaries as Hogarth, Cruickshank and Karl Marx (buried in Highgate cemetery) were regulars. Hogarth lived nearby on the site where another famous Hampstead pub, the Old Bull and Bush, now stands. The oldest rooms in the Flask have half-panelled walls, wooden armchairs and high-backed settles, an open fire and service through a sash window. Steps lead up to a later, more spacious room, which has a tiled floor, low settles and Windsor chairs, and is used as the main eating area.

The Flask is a few minutes' walk from the centre of Highgate village and has a rural atmosphere, surrounded by spacious houses and ample greenery. In warm weather, crowds of mainly young people spill out onto the large forecourt with its benches and seats. On winter evenings, the warm atmosphere and soft lighting are cosy and inviting. As with so much of Hampstread and Highgate, the Flask offers an element of sophistication and charm missing from most of the surrounding city.

The inn is linked with other Highgate taverns by the singular ceremony of the Swearing on the Horns, which involves kissing a pair of antlers tied to a pole. Those who take part are granted the freedom of Highgate if they swear to drink strong ale 'nor kiss the maid when the mistress is about but sooner than miss a chance, kiss them both.'

The Flask, Highgate, a London local with the atmosphere of a country pub

The Flask
Licensee: Bernice Chamberlain
77 Highgate,
West Hill,
London N6
☎ (01) 340 3969
11 - 3; 5.30 - 11

Ind Coope Burton Ale;
Taylor Walker Bitter

Lunchtime food every day (snacks Sunday).

Highgate and Archway stations (Northern Line)

CAMBRIDGE
NORWICH & THE FENS

East Anglia is an anachronism; a great region with a long history of religious and political struggle, close to London and yet curiously remote from it. It is that 'so near and yet so far' quality that has made it for centuries the natural country retreat of first the nobility and then the new entrepreneurial class. The rush is now on to emulate them. The population of the region is expected to double by the end of the century. However good the intentions of the newcomers – 'bleddy furriners' as they are known locally – East Anglia's ruminative charm and easy way of life is bound to change.

Yet change is nothing new. East Anglia has been at differing times the seat of kingly, ecclesiastical and temporal power. Oliver Cromwell, who lopped off a king's head and briefly established a republican commonwealth, was a man of the fens. Until the advent of the railway, ports such as Boston and King's Lynn, now pleasant backwaters, were major ports exporting to the Continent. It is no accident that there is a Boston on the east coast of the United States, for many of the first settlers in North America came from East Anglia.

The Industrial Revolution ruthlessly quashed the home-spun industries of the region. But agriculture remains and the beery delights of this book are in part made possible by the great grain basket of the eastern counties.

The relative flatness of the region – some of the land is reclaimed from the sea – makes it a comfortable place to travel. What it lacks in undulation it more than makes up for with the often startling scenery: great banks of clouds unfurling over the landscape, storm-blasted trees standing like weary sentinels on the horizon, the majesty of Ely Cathedral floating into vision over the Fens like a godly ship of state, and everywhere the promise and menace of the sea that threatens to win back what originally belonged to it.

Cambridge is a world-renowned city, one of the loftiest seats of learning. From the A1 take the Huntingdon road into the fens and along the A606 for the quick journey into this elegant but welcoming city where pedal power still rules. Its origins are ancient. It was a settlement around the River Cam before Roman times. It became a vital hub in the Roman scheme and the invaders built a bridge across the river, giving the town its name.

In spite of its scholarly associations, Cambridge was a major trading town long before the first college, Peterhouse, was built in 1284 by the Bishop of Ely. It was in that century that the collegiate system was introduced, with students living cheek by jowl with their religious and lay

Discarded fishing boats at Kings Lynn

Previous page: The uniquely named Old Bell & Steelyard, Woodbridge

masters rather than in the town itself. This exclusiveness gave rise to the division of 'town and gown' that today is a peaceful and mutually appreciative one but which in the past was the cause of anger and even violence.

It is a city of enormous charm, with the imposing colleges standing proud between Market Hill and the Cam, and lawns known as The Backs sloping gently down to the water's edge. Many medieval buildings remain in Northampton and Magdalene streets and there is an imposing hammer-beam roof in the 16th century St John's Hall. Christopher Wren built the brilliant library in Trinity College, and King's College Chapel has Ruben's Adoration of the Magi and a fifteenth-century, vaulted roof.

The Free Press, Cambridge – beware the Degradation of Drunkenness!

The pub, singled out from many fine watering holes in Cambridge, not only has its own wry history but also enthusiastically joins the disparate strands of town and gown.

Chris Lloyd's cheery little pub, packed with settles, panelled walls and much Cantabrian memorabilia, was first licensed in 1834 when a home-brewer named Sarah Horne turned her cottage into a commercial establishment. The name is facetious: at the time that Miss Sarah was setting-up in business, a local temperance paper named the Free Press railed unsuccessfully against the evils of alcohol and folded after just one issue. The tongue-in-cheek attitude is also evident in the front bar: above the open fire, on the left-hand side, are the words taken from a

The Free Press
Licensee: Chris Lloyd
Prospect Row (near Parker's Piece)
Cambridge
☎ (0223) 68337
10 - 2.30; 6 - 11

Greene King Mild (winter); IPA and Abbot

Lunchtime food. Families welcome.

tombstone warning against the Degradation of Drunkenness.

In spite of that grim upbraiding, the Free Press is a jolly, uninhibited pub, a haunt of students and cricket, rugby and rowing enthusiasts. The tiny snug at the back measures just five feet by seven and there are regular attempts to break the record of 53 people inside it.

The small pub, ranged around its central bar, is painted the regulation nicotine brown, but the right-hand section is a no-smoking zone and there is even space for a children's room. It has no juke box or insidious pool table and its appeal is so powerful that when some regulars moved to Gibraltar they opened a pub of the same name on the Rock.

You can find the Free Press easily enough from Fenner's cricket ground and the open greenery of Parker's Piece. Go up Warkworth Terrace, left into Warkworth Street and then right into Prospect Row. The slightly weary police officers in the nick are used to visitors: when you say you are looking for a pub, they give a tired grin, say, 'Yes, the Free Press' and dutifully hand you a map to help find this singular drinking haunt.

The massive inglenook at the Lattice House, Kings Lynn

Now we head north into the Fenland, along the winding A10, past Ely Cathedral and finally into the Norfolk coastal town of King's Lynn. This once dominant port was first called Bishop's Lynn and was a walled town. The walls have all but disappeared but you enter Lynn through an ancient gatehouse and pass streets of still elegant, tall houses. Some of the character of the town has been lost in the modern shopping precinct but its centrepiece, the delightful Tuesday Market Place, remains intact. Buildings worthy of a second glance include the mid-nineteenth century Corn Exchange in the Market Place, the fifteenth-century Guildhall and St Margaret's Church that dates back to the twelfth century. If you turn your back on the Corn Exchange and take one of the narrow streets off the Market Place, you arrive in Chapel Street.

The Lattice House belies its size from the outside. It is a stunning, almost unchanged fifteenth-century tavern, first built in 1487 and bequeathed to the chaplain of St Nicholas Chapel by a local merchant named Hugh Crosse. The inn remained part of the chapel estate until 1975. The pub is a series of rambling and interconnected rooms with astonishingly high ceilings, open to the rafters in parts. When it is fairly empty and quiet, there is an almost eerily medieval feel to the place as you walk the bare boards and gaze up into the dim, distant rafters.

The Lattice House
Licensee: Terry Duckett
Chapel Street,
King's Lynn,
Norfolk
☎ Kings Lynn (0553) 777292
10.30 - 2.30; 6 - 11

Everard Old Original; Greene King IPA and Abbot; Marston Pedigree (range liable to change)

Snacks lunchtime and evening (not Sunday).

The ground floor room to the left as you enter has a magnificent great inglenook, spoilt only by a mock log fire fuelled by gas. Winding stairs take you up to the Rafters Bar and balcony where the medieval feel is even stronger and you half expect to see strolling bands of lute players. It is a pity that the twentieth-century is allowed to intrude downstairs in the shape of the ubiquitous pool table, but no doubt visiting teams of archers made a nuisance of themselves in earlier times. In general, the Lattice House exudes a powerful feeling of a bygone age and is one of the last surviving genuine inns of its period in England, a showpiece of a fine town that deserves greater recognition.

Temptation – the Adam & Eve, Norwich

Norwich, on the other hand, has lost neither its fame nor its fortune. It is the dominating capital of Norfolk and is reached from King's Lynn along the bleak run of the A47. It is a city that has survived; its breathtakingly beautiful, cloistered cathedral watched over by the squat, dominating and protective Norman castle on its mound. It is a maze of alleys and cobbled ways and the new shopping area blends with rather than destroys the character. The town walls are still in evidence and once rivalled London's.

The original settlement by the River Wensum was founded by the Saxons, then later developed around the Tombland area by the Normans. Waves of later immigrants added to the industry and culture of the city. Flemish weavers were an important commercial element and the impact of artisans from Flanders and the Nord can be seen in the road named Rouen. Norwich was also a great brewing town, boasting until recent times three sturdy independents in Morgan, Bullard, and Steward & Patteson, but the arrival of Watney in the area put paid to local ale and choice, and now the beers of the 'Norwich Brewery Company' are trunked in incongruously from Halifax in Yorkshire.

This historic old tavern, older even than the city walls, is reached along Palace Street from the Norman Tombland, past the cathedral. It was built in 1249 to provide bread and ale for the workmen building the cathedral. The flint and brick walls and timber beams were joined at a later date by a Flemish gable end, which gives the present tavern an unusual but inviting aspect. The pub has a ghost, that of the hapless Lord Sheffield, who was hacked to death in the Adam and Eve in 1549 during Kett's Rebellion. In more recent times, it was a haunt of wherrymen from the Broads and the coast; a Victorian landlady named Mrs Howes also owned a wherry named the Adam and Eve and was thought to have been involved in contraband.

Baskets of flowers greet you on the terrace. There are two bars on the ground floor, including a small snug where children may sit. Steep steps take you down to the lower bar, thought to be 700 years old. There are high-backed settles, tiled and parquet floors and half-panelled walls. The Adam and Eve exudes an air of great antiquity, comfort and charm and is a perfect refreshment place after a visit to the cathedral. It is only to be regretted that its present owners do not honour both the pub's and the city's history by providing genuine Norwich beers.

There were once no less than 44 pubs in Norwich's still busy street market, a blaze of striped awnings. Only the rococo and Regency Sir Garnet remains, a three-storeyed, elegant, bow-windowed creation that rises steeply up the marketside from its raucous bottom bar to its top bar. The two bars were once separate pubs and there is a marked difference in style between them. The bottom bar is a haven for market workers and is crowded and heavy with the delightful local dialect. The ceiling is festooned with programmes from Norwich City football matches. The upper bar is quieter and more reserved, with fine views out over the bustle of the market. There are busts of both Sir Garnet Wolseley and General Gordon.

Wolseley was an Irish officer sent with an expeditionary force to Egypt to relieve Gordon. He arrived too late and the now little heard expression 'All Sir Garnet', meaning everything is all right, must surely have been facetious. This

The uniquely named Sir Garnet Wolseley. Above: anyone who supports Norwich City is in need of a drink! Opposite: 'All Sir Garnet'

The Adam and Eve
Licensee: Colin Durgess
17 Bishopgate,
Norwich
☎ Norwich (0603) 667423
10.30 - 2.30; 5.30 - 11

S&P Bitter; Ruddles County; Websters Yorkshire Bitter

Lunchtime food. Terrace drinking area. Families welcome.

The Sir Garnet Wolseley
Licensee: Colin Earthy
36 Market Place,
Norwich
☎ Norwich (0603) 615892
10.30 - 2.30; 5.30 - 11

Courage Best Bitter, Directors

Lunchtime food. Accommodation.

delightfully cheery pub is composed of once-private dwelling houses dating back to the fifteenth and seventeenth centuries and was the birthplace of the botanist Sir James Smith. The pub offers not only a good temporary resting place in central Norwich but also has more permanent accommodation with three guest rooms

It is time to change counties again; a fast journey down the A146 and A145 via Beccles brings us to Southwold on the Suffolk coast. This small, unspoilt Edwardian resort and market town has fine houses strung round its green and a long, windswept pebble beach. The

There are no excuses for failing to find the Sole Bay Inn at Southwold

The Sole Bay Inn
Licensee: John Williams
7 East Green,
Southwold,
Suffolk
☎ Southwold (0502)
723736
10.30 - 2.30; 6 - 11

Adnams Mild, Bitter, Extra

Lunchtime food. Seats on pavement.

town was destroyed by fire in the seventeenth century and carefully rebuilt and restored. Cannons stare belligerently from the cliff top to repel any invaders; they were sent to Southwold in 1745 by Charles I for protection against privateers based in Dunkirk. The town has an imposing Perpendicular church, St Edmunds, where 'Southwold Jack', a fifteenth-century oak figure of a man-at-arms, strikes the bell of the church clock. Jack also appears in the nearby Blythburgh Church and is used in promotions for Adnams' brewery, the town's major employer. Adnams brew succulent beers, which are supplied to all but one pub in Southwold. The brewery has expanded in recent years and has also turned the Crown Hotel in the High Street into the showplace for its wine business.

The Sole Bay nestles at the foot of the inshore, whitewashed lighthouse. It is a small, old-fashioned little house, Adnams' brewery tap, with a good mix of locals and visitors. Its name commemorates the battle of Sole Bay in 1672 and a British victory over the Dutch. The pub is Victorian, made up of two small houses, although the cellar is much older; a blocked-up passage is believed to have been used by smugglers who brought French brandy and other contraband up from the beach. Tiny though it is, the Sole Bay once had two bars, but they have long since been knocked into one, which currently has walls decked out with sailing prints and models of boats.

The pub is thought to have a ghost. Mr Williams, a pleasantly lugubrious host, has never seen it but he says the previous landlord had a strong rapport with it 'especially when he'd had a few!' Southwold has a string of excellent and unspoilt alehouses, but the Sole Bay Inn has pride of place: quiet, homely, expressing all that is best in the good-natured Suffolk people.

The A12 south is the Ipswich and London road, taking you close to Minsmere bird sanctuary, and then on through the ancient town of Saxmundham and past Aldeburgh and the Snape Maltings concert hall, forever associated with Benjamin Britten. Before you reach the Ipswich by-pass, turn left into Woodbridge. This old Suffolk riverside town, with tumbling, cobbled streets and many fine, timbered buildings includes a pub with one of the most unusual names in the country.

The imposing timbered building has, as its crowning glory, an original steelyard or stillyard that juts out over the steeply sloping street. It is a weighing machine that dates back to 1650. Steelyards are of Roman origin and most ports had one. Woodbridge, close to Felixstowe and Ipswich, was once an important port and the steelyard was used to weigh wagons laden with corn or skins. The tavern is even older than the steelyard, having been built in 1550. The interior is quietly impressive, with a warren of rooms, settles and panelled walls, one section set aside as an eating area.

The pub has been variously known as the Three Goats, Stillyards, Fox, Bell and Blue Bell. It was owned by the Halesworth Brewing Co until 1820, then passed to Lacons of Yarmouth, Cobbold of Ipswich and finally, Greene King of Bury St Edmunds, who are investing money in carefully bringing it up to modern standards without endangering its unique character. It is a fitting place for a glass of good ale in an area rich with Saxon and Roman history before heading back to the roar and bustle of London.

The Olde Bell and Steelyard
Licensee: Stuart Lawson
New Street,
near Market Hill,
Woodbridge
Suffolk
☎ Woodbridge (039 43) 2933
11 - 3; 5.30 (6pm in winter) - 11

Greene King IPA, Abbot

Lunchtime food. Beer garden.

THE PILGRIMS WAY & THE SOUTH COAST

Previous page: 'Live eels' in the Haunch of Venison, Salisbury, perhaps the classic town pub

Southwark, the 'south work' or bridgehead of the first stone London Bridge, constructed between 1176 and 1209, was the site of the most famous pub in English literature – the Tabard Inn. It was from here that Chaucer's pilgrims set out for Canterbury, a shrine for medieval pilgrims from all over Europe after the murder of Thomas à Becket in the Cathedral. Though the Tabard no longer exists, Southwark conceals the George Inn, which we have already visited on our travels around London. Its closeness to the starting point for Chaucer's pilgrims makes the George an all but obligatory beginning to our own, rather more secular pilgrimage. Sample the George's atmosphere once more, then take the road for Canterbury.

Almost as soon as you get beyond the straitjacket of the M25, you see the 'trademarks' of the Kent landscape – fruit trees, hop poles and oast houses. The Canterbury road, the A2, spans the River Medway, which joins the Thames at Rochester, a city with a superb Norman Castle. Charles II stayed in Restoration House on his way to London to reclaim the throne, and Charles Dickens lived at Gads Hill, looking down on the city.

The Canterbury road runs along the top of the chalk downlands that stretch well across southern England, and valleys carved into the chalk create a series of intimate landscapes. To the south lies the Weald of Kent. This is one area where hedgerow trees have not been persecuted quite as relentlessly as elsewhere in England, though not through any wave of conservationist sympathies amongst the population. The trees act as windbreaks, protecting the fruit trees and, especially, the hop vines. The forests of hop poles and the oast houses that are such familiar Kent landmarks to us, would have been completely alien to Chaucer's pilgrims, for hops were not introduced into Britain until the fifteenth century.

The Miller from Chaucer's Canterbury Tales

As you surmount a hill on the outskirts of Canterbury, the magnificent cathedral comes into view. The pub we are heading for stands in its shadow. The Romans founded Durovernum on the site of a Belgic settlement, and in 597 St Augustine founded the first cathedral there. Nothing remains of that first church, but for over a thousand years Canterbury has been foremost amongst English cathedrals, its archbishop the head of the English Church. Both the city and the cathedral were damaged by the Danes in the tenth and eleventh centuries. They also suffered during the Civil War and again in the Second World War, but the cathedral remains a magnificent sight, one that will move even philistine pub-worshippers to pause, at least momentarily, for thought, before pressing on to the next classic pub.

Park somewhere near the West Gate, a fortified gatehouse once used as the city prison. If parking proves as difficult as it usually does in ancient cities, I often derive a particularly perverse pleasure from using one pub car park and then going for a drink in a different one!

Walk up the pedestrian street, once the main London to Dover road, past the mock-Medieval Royal Museum & Free Library and Queen Elizabeth's Guest Chamber, which was once an inn dating from

The City Arms in Canterbury also has a tale to tell

1573 and has some remarkable reliefs at second floor level. Down Mercery Lane you can see the rich decoration of the Christchurch Gateway, leading to the cathedral. Down the next lane is Canterbury's classic pub – the choice is yours!

Originally known as the Angelo Castle and later the Portobello, the City Arms was described as 'the stone house within a garden' where the Bailiff of the Priory & Convent of Christ Church (the cathedral) was living in 1205. Butchery Lane has changed its name a few times, too. It was known as Sunwines Lane, then Salcocks Lane and then Angel Lane – because of the magnificent view of the Angel Steeple of the cathedral – before being given its present title. Halfway along is the tile-hung frontage of the City Arms, with a mass of flowers in its summertime window boxes.

The front part of the beamed bar is bareboarded, and at the far end there is a set of snob

The City Arms
Licensees: Les & Lindsey Coles
7 Butchery Lane,
Canterbury,
Kent
☎ Canterbury (0227) 457900
10.30 - 2.30; 6 - 11

ESTᴰ 1742

Flowers Original; Fremlins Bitter; Whitbread guest beers

Lunchtime food. Evening food until 8pm.

screens, though after the cut and etched marvels of some of the London pubs, the glass in these is a bit of a disappointment. There is a carpeted area with a fireplace and beyond it, a smaller area with another fireplace. Though Canterbury is as awash with tourists as it once was with pilgrims to the tomb of Thomas à Becket, the City Arms never seems to lose the atmosphere of a friendly town local.

When you have seen the white cliffs, find the White Horse, Dover

After sating yourself with the splendours of Canterbury, take the Dover road. When traversing the Weald of Kent it is important to be fully aware of the exact difference between a 'man of Kent' and a 'Kentish man'. Unfortunately, despite years of patient explanation by Kent (or is it Kentish?) acquaintances, I can never remember the difference, and, speaking as a Yorkshireman (or is it a man of York?), the absence of such knowledge has yet to cause me much regret – they're all southerners to me!

When you near Dover, follow the signs to the docks and the road will sweep you in on a curve between the harbour and the majestic castle on a cliff top high above the town. The white cliffs are a famous landmark both to Britons returning from abroad, and to foreign visitors braving the land that invented motorway service station food, many years before the invention of motorways.

Though William the Conqueror made his landfall further along the coast at Hastings, Dover has been pounded by a series of other invaders and would-be invaders down the centuries. It was the landing site of Caesar's legions and the Roman Pharos (lighthouse) still stands within the castle walls. Angles, Saxons and Jutes all ravaged the town, which also saw action against the Spanish Armada. More recently, it was badly damaged by bombardment in both world wars; St James Church was never rebuilt after being bombed in the Second World War, though its ruins still stand and provide a useful landmark to the Dover classic pub.

You will find the White Horse at the foot of the Castle Hill, just on the harbour side of Castle Street. Enter up a couple of steps from the street and you are immediately awash on a sea of nautical memorabilia, including the Dover Rowing Club's prodigious collection of trophies. The bar serves a number of rooms, all with that archetypal sepia colouring that age and tobacco smoke impart to pubs. The main bar bends around the entrance porch and there is an alcove behind the bar, with a pool room and another small room, both up a couple more steps. A flight of even more steps leads you up to the raised garden, with honeysuckle and

The White Horse Inn
Licensee: Charles Willett
St James Street,
Dover,
Kent
☎ Dover (0304) 202911
10.30 - 2.30; 6.30 - 11

ESTᴰ 1742

Flowers Original; Fremlins Bitter; Whitbread guest beers

Lunchtime & evening food. Families welcome. Garden.

Russian vine growing over the walls. To one side is the masonry of the ruined St James Church.

The pub was built in 1365, the year that 'the sea washed the font of St James Church' alongside it. It passed out of the ownership of the church in 1539, during Henry VIII's dissolution of the monasteries, and was for many years the home of the 'ale conner' of Dover. This vital office must have been almost as eagerly sought as the editorship of the Good Beer Guide, for the ale conner's arduous official duties were to visit the Dover pubs checking the quality of the ale and making sure that none were operating a bawdy house on the side.

Sad to say, the job no longer exists, though many dedicated amateurs no doubt maintain the tradition quite voluntarily. One other tradition connected with the pub is also sadly extinct. It used to open at five in the morning for the benefit of dockworkers and others on the night shift, but those attempting to rouse Charles Willett from his slumbers for a dawn reviver are unlikely to be served, though they may pick up some colourful additions to their vocabulary.

The White Horse is definitely not a place for your white tie and tails. Its decor has seen better days, but the threadbare carpet and peeling wallpaper seem to augment rather than detract from the character and atmosphere of the pub. In a town that has witnessed more exits and entrances than a stagehand at the Old Vic, the White Horse is reassuringly constant and unchanging, a solid local pub with a welcome for all of its diverse collection of regulars.

As well as the Roman Pharos, Dover Castle contains St Edmunds Chapel, the smallest chapel in England, and much else besides. The size and thickness of the castle fortifications gives an indication of the importance of the harbour at Dover, the largest of the Cinque Ports. We shall pass several of the other ones, as we follow the south coast west towards our next classic pub, in another historic harbour town, Portsmouth.

Rye is one obligatory calling point along the way, its houses and winding streets scrabbling up the rock jutting out of the Romney Marshes. Another Cinque Port, it earned its living as much from smuggling as from legitimate seafaring, and its magnificent pub, the Mermaid, home-base of the notorious Hawkhurst gang, would certainly have been included in this book had it not already appeared in *Classic Country Pubs*.

Further along the coast is Hastings, another Cinque Port with an appropriately named, and excellent pub, the Cinque Ports, in All Saints Street. The opportunity to call for a refreshing drink is probably too good to miss, for Portsmouth is still a long way off. Just inland is Battle, where the Battle of Hastings actually took place. The Abbey was built by William the Conqueror in gratitude for his victory.

Along the coast are a succession of seaside resorts, each with its own distinctive character. Beyond the genteel town of Eastbourne lies Beachy Head, a 500-foot chalk cliff with a stomach-churning view onto the lighthouse below, for those brave enough to risk a look. Next is the brash and breezy resort of Brighton, where the ornate pleasure domes of the Royal Pavilion are compulsory viewing. I'd like to suggest a classic pub, but I haven't found one there yet; either there isn't one, or it's extremely well-hidden.

Beyond Worthing, the road runs inland towards the stately city of Chichester, still laid out on the Roman plan, with four straight streets intersecting at the centre, where there is a fine sixteenth-century market cross. See the cathedral and the Roman palace at Fishbourne, then press on to Portsmouth, where you can scale the heights and plumb the depths of our naval traditions – it is a fair bet that Frank Crocker's ancestors were involved in the design of the Mary Rose!

Portsmouth was developed as a garrison town and guardian of the Channel by Henry VII in the fifteenth century, becoming the home of the Royal Navy, complete with docks and workshops. Nelson's flagship *Victory*, HMS *Warrior* and the remains of the *Mary Rose* are all housed in the docks. Portsmouth was the birthplace of two famous literary figures, Charles Dickens and Arthur Conan Doyle, and the great designer and builder Isambard Kingdom Brunel was also born there, close to the pub of our choice.

The George is the last surviving eighteenth-century tavern in the city. Don't be put off by the more recent, plain Victorian front. Once inside you are almost overwhelmed by the rich atmosphere and the naval artefacts, including paintings of Nelson and a collection of ships' caps behind the long wooden bar. There are ships' plaques on the walls and ships' bells warn that drinking time is coming to an end; one cluster of lights is even built into a ship's wheel. Towards the rear of the single-roomed bar, formerly two separate buildings, there is a well which once stood in the courtyard between the two buildings.

When the pub was being knocked into its present shape in the last century, timbers were

The George
Licensees: John Goodall & Denis Mort
84 Queen Street,
Portsea,
Portsmouth,
Hampshire
☎ Portsmouth (0705) 821040
10 - 2.30; 7 - 10.30 (11 in summer)

EST.D 1742

Flowers Original; Fuller ESB; Gale HSB; Greene King Abbott; Whitbread Pompey Royal; Warrior Ale

Lunchtime food, including hot special dish.

The George in Portsmouth – a landlocked embodiment of the city's naval traditions

in plentiful supply in the dockyards, as the age of sail was coming to an end. The beams in the ceiling came from the yards and one is inscribed with the name of its ship, the *Ariadne*.

The George is the ideal base for visiting the *Warrior*, the *Victory* and the *Mary Rose* and is across the road from the Maritime Heritage Museum. The pub is run as a free house with a range of beers that includes a 'house brew', Warrior Ale, from the Sussex Brewery. Messrs Goodall and Mort have also acquired the building next door, which will become a restaurant with five bedrooms for guests upstairs.

Take the motorway towards Southampton and then the A33 carries you to one of the most remarkable of all cities in England, Winchester. This ancient town, with its stubby cathedral, castle remains and college, is so steeped in history that even modern chain shops are housed in listed buildings and entering Barclays Bank is akin to visiting the Parthenon! History is at every turn, in a town developed as the fifth largest in England by the Romans and declared to be the fledgling nation's capital by the Saxons. Egbert was crowned the first King of England here in 827 and Winchester was developed into a flourishing centre by Alfred the Great. William the Conqueror was crowned in both London and Winchester and declared both places to be the capitals of England. In the thirteenth century it was still England's second city, but it went into decline following its seizure by Cromwell during the Civil War.

The Bell
Licensee: Alan Riggs
85 St Cross Road (A333),
Winchester,
Hampshire
☎ Winchester (0962)
65284
10.30 - 2.30; 6 - 10.30 (11
in summer)

Marston Mercian Mild,
Burton Bitter, Pedigree

Lunchtime snacks. Large
beer garden at rear with play
area for children.

A little way out of the centre there is a small community based around the St Cross Hospital, a community that includes the delightful little pub, the Bell.

The Bell dates back to the late fourteenth century and was once owned by the Mayor of Winchester. It is now a plain, unadorned boozer, one of the last of its breed. It has lost its gable ends and its original beams are buried under the rendering, but what it lacks in architectural interest it makes up for with its cheery good nature. The public bar is a large room with flagstoned floors. The serving area is to the right, and the darts, dominoes and whist area to the left, with a large fireplace that has recently been opened up. A little passage leads to the lounge bar, comfortably furnished with banquettes and with a collection of two thousand miniature bottles in cabinets on the walls.

In the garden at the rear you can trace with ease the extensions to the building that have taken place over the centuries. St Cross Hospital, behind the pub, is the oldest charity in England. It was endowed in 1136 by Bishop Henry of Blois for thirteen poor monks. The present pensioners are still entitled to their alms of 'a horn of beer and a crust of bread'. Brewing has long since ceased on the site, though, and the inhabitants enjoy their Marston's ale in the warmth of the Bell. Beyond the hospital lie pretty water meadows and the sudden, surprising mound of St Catherine's Hill, surmounted by a maze. The St Cross community is a pleasing mixture of ancient and modern, linked together by its happy-go-lucky alehouse.

The sign of a fine local – the Bell, Winchester

The approach to Salisbury, across the border from Hampshire into Wiltshire, is along the A30, through a series of charming, sunny villages. You turn a final corner and there is one of the greatest, throat-catching glories of English architecture, the soaring cathedral started in 1220 on a bend of the Avon. The graceful tower was completed in 1334 and at four hundred feet, is the highest church tower in the land. The interior is rich in Purbeck marble and there is a great run of sun-filled cloisters, with saints smiling benignly from every niche. Salisbury is not just a cathedral, though. There is a friendly, busy, open-air market and a plethora of fine old buildings. Across the road from the ancient Poultry Cross, site of an old chicken market, is a tavern that threatens to claim the title of *the* classic pub of all England.

The Haunch, with its black-beamed and white-painted, three-storey exterior, is a no-nonsense alehouse. The building dates back to 1320 and was built, like the Adam and Eve in

Haunch of Venison
Licensees: Antony & Victoria Leroy
Minster Street,
Salisbury,
Wiltshire
☎ Salisbury (0722) 22024
10 - 2.30; 6 - 11

Courage Best Bitter and Directors

Bar food, lunch and evening restaurant.

Opposite: Getting down to brass taps – the Haunch of Venison, Salisbury

distant Norwich, to offer sustenance to the workers engaged in building the church of St Thomas – which towers over the rear of the pub. As you come in from Minster Street you enter the smallest bar in Salisbury, a handsome panelled room with an enormous fireplace. To the right is the tiny serving area, with four hand-pumps and a bank of taps that serves fortified wines and spirits by gravity from casks above the bar. The dispenser was installed by a local plumber at the turn of the century for the then owner, Bradbeer, a wine and spirit merchant. To the side of the serving area is a minuscule snug that was once a ladies' room.

A few steps lead up to a quieter, dimly lit room with another imposing fireplace and beamed ceiling. It is known as the House of Lords as it was once used by bishops, who wanted some repose from the hoi polloi in the bar below. There is a cabinet of clay pipes by the fireplace and, rather grimly, a replica of a mummified hand discovered in the pub, is set behind glass in the fireplace. The upstairs rooms are used as the restaurant and the fine room to the left was formerly part of the house next door, owned by an Elizabethan merchant. It has yet another sumptuous fireplace. The room to the right, the main restaurant area, has some original panelling, a fire certificate of 1836 and a splendid view of the medieval Poultry Cross. The Haunch of Venison is haunted by the ghost of a young woman who is never seen but whose presence is felt by the smell of flowers. Here is a wonderful and unspoilt tavern, a fittingly bibulous salute to the great city in which it stands.

The highest church tower in the land – Salisbury

Follow the A30 west to Shaftesbury, an old Saxon hill town on the Dorset/Wiltshire border. Hardy called it Shaston, and in Jude the Obscure he spoke of it as 'the city of a dream' with 'a unique position on the summit of a steep and imposing scarp . . . Its situation rendered water the great want of the town; and within living memory, horses, donkeys and men may have been seen toiling up the winding ways to the top of the height, laden with tubs and barrels filled from the wells beneath the mountain.'

Water is now in plentiful supply in Shaftesbury but it remains a largely unspoilt old town with astonishing views out over the sweep of Wessex from the promenade in front of the abbey ruins, and the sturdy old thirteenth-century church in the main street. Shaftesbury has lost many of its pubs but a goodly clutch remain, with pride of place going to the Ship Inn.

Ron May, a former lorry driver, and his wife Anne offer a genuinely warm welcome at this

The Ship Inn
Licensee: Ronald May
Bleke Street,
Shaftesbury,
Dorset
☎ Shaftesbury (0747) 3219
10.30 - 2.30; 6.30 - 11

Badger Best Bitter,
Tanglefoot

Food lunchtime & evening including hot dishes. Small garden at rear and a few seats at the front.

fine house on the corner of Bleke Street and the steep plunge of Tout Hill. The greystone building with its imposing chimneys has almost a Scottish air about it. The entrance is down a side alley, which takes visitors into a small passageway and a tiny room facing the bar. The building dates back to 1605 but it has been a pub only since the 1930s. Before that it was a doctor's house; the first room as you enter was once the patients' waiting room, while the large lounge restaurant to the left was the consulting room.

The link between the surgery and the pub was the doctor, a member of the Matthews family who ran a small brewery in nearby Gillingham (pronounced with a hard G to distinguish

A new use for old consulting rooms... the Ship Inn, Shaftesbury

it from its Kentish namesake). When he retired, it seemed a sensible step to turn the house into a public one dispensing good cheer rather than medicinal compounds. Matthews were taken over by Hall and Woodhouse who supply the Ship with their nutty ales from Blandford Forum.

The former consulting room turned lounge/ restaurant has elegant panelling and a splendid fireplace surmounted by a fine clock. It is linked to the taproom by the bar, behind which a striking staircase rises to the Mays' private rooms, jugs hang from a beam and there are notes of many currencies pinned to the wall. The bar curves round at the end of a short passage to serve the small tap room, while a few steps take you down to a more modern room occupied by a pool table, necessary no doubt, but sadly out of keeping with the surroundings.

Much of the panelling came from a demolished pub on the other side of Bleke Street called . . . the Ship. The doctor's house took the name when it adopted its new role in the 1930s. The present Ship is no Bleke House but has an air of unforced, sturdy welcome, serving excellent, tasty ale and simple food.

BATH & THE WEST COUNTRY

Having seen the deep south, we are now heading west, out along the M4, past Heathrow Airport and the obligatory tourist calling point of Windsor, with its rather less obligatory sister town of Slough, for which John Betjeman coined the immortal lines: 'Come friendly bombs and rain on Slough!'

Give both of them a miss on this trip and instead stray north off the motorway for a few miles to call at Henley, home of the famous regatta on the river, but more important for our present purposes, home also of the estimable Brakspear's brewery, whose products I recommend you to sample in any of the many excellent Henley pubs, but especially in the Three Tuns.

A long, tiled corridor runs the length of the pub, leading to a terrace with wooden benches and flower tubs, and a Coke machine to keep the children supplied while you are trying out some of the excellent range of Brakspear's beers. At the front is a small public bar with an old brick fireplace and a boarded ceiling; the locals and the liveliest conversation tend to be found in here. Across the bar is the oak-beamed Buttery, dominated by a huge central fireplace. Beyond it is a small dining area, with a mural of an improbable looking dray-horse.

The Three Tuns has been open all day for a number of years, anticipating the changes in licensing laws by serving tea and coffee outside permitted hours. It now has a restaurant licence, allowing it to serve alcohol throughout the day to those eating 'a substantial meal'. The Knowles have resisted the temptation to round up their food prices, so this is one of the few eating places in Great Britain where you may find yourself paying 67 pence or £4.81, or any odd numbers in between, for your food!

Henley is not an easy place to leave during licensing hours. If you can manage to do so, either head south for Reading and the M4 or take a more leisurely route westwards through the Chilterns, admiring the countryside and the many excellent country pubs it contains, before picking up the M4 to the next calling point, the Bear at Hungerford. Turn off the M4 at junction 14 and follow the Hungerford signs south. Turn right at the T-junction onto the A4, and, when you reach the mini-roundabout, you will see the Bear in front of you.

The Bear dates from the thirteenth century and has seen its share of famous patrons over the years. Samuel Pepys and John Evelyn both mention a stay at the Bear in their diaries, Pepys praising 'the very good trout'. When Celia Fiennes, the famous traveller, visited the town

The Three Tuns
Licensees: Jack & Gillian Knowles
5 Market Place,
Henley-on-Thames
Oxfordshire
☎ Henley (0491) 573260
10 - 11; Sunday 12 - 10.30

Brakspear's Mild, Bitter, Special, Old

Food available all day. Restaurant licence. Outdoor drinking area.

The Three Tuns, Henley – Brakspear country on the edge of Shakespeare country

Previous page: Stained glass in the Coeur de Lion, Bath

she remarked that the town was 'famous for crayfish, there being a good river and great quantetys of that fish and large'. John of Gaunt granted fishing rights on the Kennet to ninety-nine householders or 'Tuttimen' in the fourteenth century, and their descendants still gather on Easter Tuesday to parade their 'tutties' or nosegays, steal kisses from those women who take their fancy and drink toasts to the 'immortal memory of John of Gaunt'.

Charles I had his Civil War headquarters at the Bear for a while, and in December 1688, William, Prince of Orange, stayed there while negotiating with commissioners acting for James II. Shortly afterwards James fled to France, leaving his throne to William and Mary.

William Bell, the landlord of the Bear at the time, was one of five issuers of trade tokens (the illegal, but very widespread coinage used in England, Wales and Ireland in the seventeenth century) in Hungerford. In 1685 he was paid eight shillings (forty pence) for a barrel of beer used in a celebration of the Duke of Monmouth's defeat at the battle of Sedgemoor. These days that would not even buy you a half-pint in the bar!

The Bear bar is beamed and timbered with an open fire blazing in a brick fireplace. The day's newspapers hang on reading-sticks and the choice of titles – *International Herald Tribune, Financial Times* and *Sporting Life* – gives a fair idea of the clientele at this three-star hotel. There is a stuffed bear in a glass case alongside the bar and a fine Marsh and Highworth clock, and through an archway is an eating area with candles and fresh flowers on the tables.

French windows open onto a courtyard with flower tubs in summer and a fountain, and there is also a riverside garden. A wide range of excellent bar meals includes Hungerford trout (though not the one that Pepys praised!) and vegetarian dishes. All the ingredients are fresh, and all the cheeses are unpasteurised English farmhouse cheeses. More substantial meals can be taken in the restaurant, either from the five-course House menu or the six-course Gourmet menu. Prices are not cheap, but quality is excellent.

You could follow the Kennet & Avon Canal west from Hungerford to our next destination, Bath, but those who have not had the forethought to arrange a narrow boat, may be better advised to stick to the M4.

From junction 18 of the M4, the A46 takes you to the outskirts of Bath. Turn into town along the A4 and stick with it. Eventually, a mile or so from the city centre the road forks right to become the 'through route'.

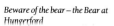

Beware of the bear – the Bear at Hungerford

The Bear Inn
Licensee: Roy Tudor-Hughes
Charnham Street,
Hungerford,
Berkshire
☎ Hungerford (0488) 82512
11 - 2.30; 6 - 11

Arkell BB, BBB; Morland Bitter

Lunchtime & evening food. Restaurant. Accommodation. Families welcome if dining. Garden.

At this stage it is known as The Vineyards and is lined by Georgian terraces. On your right, modestly advertising its presence, is the Star Inn.

Bath is in the first division of British tourist towns, providing not only its famous sites but a full range of interesting, good value accommodation, restaurants and pubs. Its heritage of elegant houses comes from three hundred years of being the upper crust's favourite summer retreat. Simply walking the streets is fascinating in itself. Many still come with the prime purpose of visiting the ancient Roman hot spring baths that gave the city its name and the gothic abbey next door, which gave it an architectural centrepiece and geographical reference point.

The Star Inn
Licensee: Alan Perrett
23 Vineyards,
Bath,
Avon
☎ Bath (0225) 25072
10.30 - 2.30; 5.30 - 10.30
(11 Friday & Saturday)

Draught Bass; Guest beers

The Star Inn, Bath – apparently unchanged for a hundred years

Before you venture into the city itself stop awhile at the Star. Every town should have a pub like this, but alas, few have.

The layout of bars would appal modern brewery architects, whose blinkered vision created the monotonous, characterless, single-lounge-bar, alcohol dispense units that have replaced Britain's pub heritage. The Star has a small, sedate lounge with its own bar, manned at times when the bar staff are not by the fire chatting with the customers. The public end has three small rooms and is served from a large bar backed by half-a-dozen stillaged barrels. There can be few better ways to serve Draught Bass than straight from a barrel that has lain long enough to mature.

The pub is wood-panelled throughout and appears to have remained unchanged for a hundred years. There is a huge flower pot overseeing proceedings, and only the toilets are furnished to modern standards. On a Friday night visit the average age of the customers was sixty, with a light smattering of respectful youth. The settles were lined with portly gentlemen whose faces revealed complete familiarity with their surroundings and with their fellows. I asked one old chap how long he had been drinking at the Star: 'Since about seven-thirty, mate,' he grinned.

This is a pub of a type that I am convinced many people want and that brewery planners should study for future reference. No muzak, no fruit machines, no electronic beeper games, no smell of chips and burned burgers, no loud advertisements for this month's major promotion. Just the eternal hubbub of conversation, the chink of glass on glass and hosts who know their profession well.

On leaving the Star you will need to go back 100 yards along The Vineyards to the road junction that directs you to the city centre. Persevere until you reach Bath Abbey, by which time you will have gone a wee bit too far but will in any case need to park. Our next classic pub, The Coeur de Lion, lies in a shopping arcade at the back of High Street. To be precise, it is behind J.W. Crooks & Sons, clothiers, of number 21.

I have always been wary of recommending the Coeur de Lion to pub connoisseurs because although its setting, in a flower-basketed mews area filled with small shops, is pleasant enough and its stained glass façade is particularly attractive, its interior has been shabby and poorly maintained for many years. What persuades me to include it here are the plans of its new tenants, Gill and Steve Shewring.

The Coeur de Lion is as Georgian as the rest of Bath's central area. It is believed originally to have been a coffee house, converting to a pub 150 years ago. It is one of the contenders in the long-standing battle to be the smallest pub in Britain and in my view, it comes second only to the Nutshell in Bury St Edmunds, if one is measuring just the drinking area.

When the Shewrings took over they came to the same conclusions as I did about the khaki baize walls, boring furnishings, and plywood bar. Their aim is to return it as closely as possible to its original Georgian state. At the time of my visit, the process of revealing the original stone walls, furnishing it with eighteenth-century pews and designing a more suitable bar, was well advanced. I hope they will also make a feature of the metal pillars that have assisted the building in staying upright all these years.

Northumberland Place was named after the Earl of Northumberland who owned the land

The Coeur de Lion
Licensees: Gillian & Steve Shewring
Northumberland Place,
Off High Street,
Bath,
Avon
☎ Bath (0225) 65371
10.30 - 2.30; 5.30 - 10.30
(11 Friday & Saturday)

Cornish Dry Hop Bitter;
Wessex Stud

Lunchtime & evening
snacks. Small garden.

on which the mews area was built. It makes an ideal starting point for an afternoon of more traditional tourist pursuits, if you can avoid the temptation of sampling the range of bottled 'steam brewery' beer.

Fifteenth-century craftsmanship, still delights twentieth-century visitors at the George & Pilgrim Hotel, Glastonbury

The A39 Wells road out of Bath begins life as the A4 west to Bristol. Just out of town it branches south and starts its journey through Somerset. Glastonbury is ten miles beyond Wells and our next classic pub lies in its main street.

I doubt that Major Richardson has ever thought of his splendid residential inn as a pub, but a fully licensed house it is and so qualifies for inclusion here. The George & Pilgrims took twenty years to complete back in the fifteenth century, presumably because of the skilled craftsmanship demanded from the stone masons who were responsible for its construction. It fits in splendidly with the rest of this affable and affluent market town, steeped in millennia of history.

Glastonbury was supposed to be the birthplace of Christianity in the British Isles and has a seventh-century abbey to prove it. More recently, a new generation of religious enthusiasts have claimed that it was the spiritual home of pagan pre-Christian beliefs, and so it has a midsummer folk festival to support this idea. The residents tend to be keener on the former than the latter.

Whatever your chosen version of history, the antique charm of the George & Pilgrims' front bar will impress you. The mullioned windows with carved stone surrounds, the genuinely old furnishings, the iron gates that can close off the bar, and the more recent mantelpiece above the open fire, all conspire to evoke historical fantasies from the most hardened traveller.

If you prefer more of a 'local' atmosphere, then the back (Monks') bar will oblige. You can play shove ha'penny here, which is always a good sign, in what is essentially a smart hotel catering to the richer end of the tourist market.

Staying at the George & Pilgrims is expensive by West Country standards but guests will be rewarded by a first-rate menu and a room that comes straight from an historical novel. There are three four-poster beds and one 'half-tester' amongst the eight bedrooms in the older part of the hotel. Even if you choose not to stay, the bar food can be recommended.

When you leave Glastonbury, carry on along the A39, which will eventually bring you to the M5 at junction 18. Our next classic pub is forty miles to the south, off junction 30 at Exeter. There you should fol-

The George & Pilgrims Hotel
Licensees: Major & Mrs Jack Richardson
High Street, Glastonbury, Somerset
☎ Glastonbury (0458) 31146
11 - 2.30; 6 - 11

Draught Bass

Lunchtime & evening food. Restaurant Monday - Saturday. Snacks all week. Families welcome. Garden. Accommodation.

low the signs to Marsh Barton, Exeter's largest trading estate. From that point, directions become farcical.

Find the city incinerator in the bowels of the estate: it is the tallest of the chimneys and fairly well signposted. To the left of its main entrance is a tarmac track winding its way over a small bridge. This is marked as a 'no through road', but carry on to its end, which involves crossing a wooden swingbridge and motoring along the canal towpath. You will need faith but the effort is well worth it!

The double canal locks from which the pub takes its name are part of the Exeter ship canal, the oldest inland waterway in the United King-

A traditional pub game in a fine traditional pub – The Double Locks, Exeter

The Double Locks
Licensee: Jamie Stuart
Canal Banks,
Alphington,
Exeter
☎ Exeter (0392) 56947
11 - 2.30; 5.30 - 10.30 (11
Friday & Saturday)

Eldridge Pope Royal Oak;
Everards Old Original
(summer); Golden Hill
Exmoor Ale; Marston
Pedigree, Owd Rodger;
Wadworth 6X; Old Timer
(winter)

Lunchtime food, 11 - 2 all
week. Evening food, 5.30 -
10 all week. Families
welcome. Garden.

dom. Built in the sixteenth century, it used to carry cargo vessels up to the town from the English channel, but nowadays it operates for small pleasure craft. Sitting on the canal bank feels like being in the heart of the English countryside, though you are in fact surrounded on all sides by the expanding city of Exeter. The site is part of a conservation area.

The Double Locks is the creation of Jamie Stuart, an ex-farmer who looks, sounds and motors like an unbearded Devonian Richard Branson. When he bought the place in 1983 it was in a sorry state of disrepair. It was the only pub he had ever considered owning and since that time he has been ploughing most of his considerable energies into helping it reach its potential. He is that rare commodity, an entrepreneurial small businessman with abundant good taste.

Breakfast is served at eleven and for the price

The Double Locks with one of its namesakes

of a croissant in some local hotels you can have a full English fry-up and the pint of your choice. You may care to take it in the conservatory or sit among the stuffed animals and model boats in the splendidly 'lived-in' saloon bar, complete with its bar billiards table.

Many drinkers simply stand in the corridor that dissects the pub. Others prefer the plain but strongly atmospheric public bar; its servery is dominated by the backdrop of a score of barrels, stacked one on another, each serving a well-kept pint direct to the glass.

Outside there are tables by the locks and a large, safe, children's play area crammed with things to climb on. There are facilities for volleyball and badminton too. The converted cowshed acts as a function room for private parties and as an overflow bar in summer if the garden is crowded.

At weekends in the season there is a barbecue outdoors. Otherwise the regular lunchtime and evening food comes from an extensive menu, all home-prepared to a high standard. Features include a good vegetarian selection and a range of traditional British pies.

The range of ales is impressive. The ciders are real Devonian, rather than fermented French apple juice, and come from Gray's cider farm at nearby Tedburn St Mary. The wine list is above the pub average and even the selection of Irish whiskies is noteworthy. One wonders what it will be like when it is completely finished!

The final pub on our tour to the West Country lies forty miles to the south-west in Plymouth. Whilst it is probably the least impressive of the pubs in this section, it lies in the most interesting area, the waterfront area of The Barbican.

I will leave you in the hands of Exeter's road-sign writers to find your way to the A38 westwards. As in many expanding modern cities they are overly keen to direct visitors away and on to other destinations. The dual carriageway reaches Plymouth at the Marsh Mills roundabout, where you should turn left past the Bass depot and follow signs to the city centre. After a mile and a half, The Barbican is indicated to your left off Exeter Street. As you follow the road round, Looe Street is to your right. Parking may require imagination.

Plymouth is a city port. It has housed a naval station and dockyard for nearly five hundred years and as a result was heavily bombed during the Second World War. Much of its centre was destroyed and the piecemeal planning of the post-war years left many of the modern areas without character. By a miracle, however, the

The Minerva
Licensee: John Weston
Looe Street,
Barbican,
Plymouth
☎ Plymouth (0752) 669065
11 - 3; 6.30 - 11

Courage Best Bitter

Lunchtime food. Pasties & rolls only.

traditional harbourside quarter of The Barbican was virtually untouched by either onslaught.

The Minerva was built in 1555 and for many years was part of 'Millionaires' Row', a cobbled street lined by merchants' houses. Nowadays the monolithic façades often hide decaying inner city interiors. The cobbled streets give a mews feel to the place and the partially pedestrianised area on the waterfront is awash with increasingly impressive and expensive restaurants, antique shops and the like. The council commissioned Lenkiewicz, a local painter, to brighten the streets with exotic murals, as tall as houses. But there is squalor, too, and the oldest types of harbour trades.

The pub is a simple place. The front drinking area wraps itself around a plain bar which in turn is built around four casks of Best Bitter, draped in Union Jack tea towels. The above-average ale is served straight from the barrel. The back room is stone-walled and boasts a blackened stove and a dartboard. The seafaring connections are plentiful.

Purists fume at the sight of beams painted black, but it is the way they have always done it in Plymouth. At least the beams are original. With the smoke-stained walls and simple furnishings they give this friendly pub a well-used, cosy feel. The customers are not so sleepy though. Last year they won the first two places in the south-western quiz league.

My guess is that in a few years the Barbican will be 'gentrified' and that 'yachty yuppies' will walk its polished alleyways arm in arm in search of expensive French cuisine. And what of this simple pub then? Enjoy it while you can.

The Minerva, Plymouth – find it before the 'yachty yuppies' do!

WALES &
THE WELSH MARCHES

We shall travel no further into the south-west than Plymouth on this journey. Those needing a respite from the rigours of pub-going may want to spend a while wandering through Devon and Cornwall, those made of sterner stuff will make a fast journey back up the M5 before taking the M4 and the suspension bridge over the Severn and into Wales. We shall travel up through the Welsh borders shortly; for now, make for Cardiff and its remarkable Victorian pub, the Golden Cross.

If you are arriving in Cardiff by train, turn right as you come out of the station and walk down Saunders Road and along Custom House Street to the Golden Cross. By car from the M4/M48 take the road in past the castle, then turn left down High Street, keep straight on down St Mary Street and Custom House Street is on the left at the bottom. If you can negotiate the back streets under the railway successfully, there is an NCP car park directly across the road from the Golden Cross.

Like London's magnificent Black Friar, the Golden Cross was saved from demolition only by an energetic campaign by its regulars and by admirers of its superb Victorian features. A road-widening scheme flattened every other building in the area, but the knights of the Golden Cross organised petitions, secured a Grade II listing as a building of outstanding architectural merit and won the battle to save it. The pub remained as an island in a sea of demolition; drivers now negotiate a gentle dog-leg around it.

Its green and gold tiled façade is a stunning sight, particularly at night, when it is floodlit. The Victorian Golden Cross is in marked contrast to its giant modern neighbours, particularly the Holiday Inn which dwarfs it, but the pub loses nothing in the comparison.

The tilework continues inside the Golden Cross with tiled walls including inset murals of Cardiff Castle and the old Town Hall, but the outstanding feature is the magnificent curved, tile-fronted bar. The pub has been lovingly restored and original features such as the mahogany bar fittings are unobtrusively blended with newer additions. Off the main bar are a plush lounge, a small, comfortable snug and a dining area with a superb Victorian cast-iron fireplace.

The lunchtime food is all home-made from fresh ingredients and the emphasis is on traditional British cooking, with Beef in Brains (the beer, not the grey matter) a particular speciality. If the weather is fine, there is a paved area outside where you can sit and drink a toast to the campaigners who saved this magnificent pub from a premature burial beneath the road which now skirts it.

When you have washed the travel dust from

The superb tiled bar in the Golden Cross, Cardiff

Previous page: Appropriate decor from the Boathouse, Shrewsbury

The Golden Cross
Licensees: Adrian & Karin Price
Hayesbridge Road,
Custom House Street,
Cardiff,
South Glamorgan
11 - 3; 5.30 - 11

Brain Dark, Bitter, SA.

Lunchtime food. Paved outside drinking area. Families welcome in dining area.

your throat with a glass or two of Brains' excellent beer (the Dark is a particular pleasure), take a wander through the city centre and have a look round the Castle. Then, if the weather is fine, take a riverside stroll to a pub that offers a total contrast to the decorative splendours of the Golden Cross, but has just as warm a welcome.

Walk up Castle Street and take the footpath to your right immediately after you have crossed the Taff. The footpath follows the river bank out past Sophia Gardens, where Glamorgan play much of their cricket, and then winds its way to the historic city of Llandaff, where you will find a superb cathedral, a ruined castle, an ancient wall and an excellent local pub.

The homely interior of the Butcher's Arms, Llandaff
Below: The Butcher's Arms – fourteen centuries of Welsh history can be traced in Llandaff

If the weather is less than good or you cannot be tempted into parting with your car, take Cathedral Road (A4119) out of Cardiff and turn right in Llandaff by the Maltsters and the Black Lion. The Butchers Arms is halfway up the High Street on the left. You should be able to park at the top of the hill, where you are equidistant from cathedral, castle, well and pub; the order in which you visit them is entirely a matter between you and the licensing laws.

The home-spun, lived-in interior of the Butchers Arms is a stark contrast to that of the Golden Cross. It would not win any design awards, but it offers further proof that the essence of a good pub is as much to do with character, atmosphere and the quality of the licensees as a myriad architectural delights.

The Butchers Arms was once a butcher's shop. It is now an unspoilt and very friendly local pub, though the excellence of the home-cooked ham is a fitting tribute to its former use. The central bar serves a tiny front bar with a dartboard and a lounge area, and at the back of the pub there is a lounge/dining area. A glass case full of bottled celebration ales indicates the landlord's interest in beer. If further proof is needed, the quality of his Draught Bass will provide it; Llandaff is a long way from Burton upon Trent, but the Bass has certainly lost nothing on the journey.

The Golden Cross and The Butchers Arms

Butchers Arms
Licensee: C.D. Williams
High Street,
Llandaff,
Cardiff
☎ Cardiff (0222) 561898
11 - 3; 5.30 - 11

Draught Bass; Hancocks HB

Lunchtime food.

are at opposite ends of the spectrum of town pubs, one a glamorous piece of architectural heritage, the other an unpretentious vernacular building, but in terms of their value to their communitities and their regulars, both are equally important. If you like pubs, you will appreciate the special qualities of them both.

At the top of the High Street you will find the ruins of Bishop's Castle, a fortified residence built in 1266-87 and damaged during the Owain Glyndwr's War of Independence from 1401-5. Just along the road is the Cathedral Green, from where you can look down onto the magnificent Llandaff Cathedral, founded in the sixth century by St Teilo. Most of the present building dates from the twelfth and thirteenth centuries, though a part of it was rebuilt after Second World War bomb damage. Llandaff also has a thirteenth-century Preaching Cross, mentioned by Geoffrey of Monmouth, where the Crusades were preached, and, down the lane that leads to the Cathedral is St Teilo's Well.

After the castles of Cardiff and Llandaff, one other in the area must be mentioned. Signposted off the A470 north of Cardiff, Castell Coch is sited on the ruins of a genuine medieval castle, but is actually a Victorian fantasy of incredible extravagance. Architect William Burges, backed by the prodigious wealth of Lord Bute, created a castle that would be more at home in Transylvania than on a wooded Welsh hillside, with interior decoration of stunning opulence – vaulted ceilings, fantastic murals, even a dungeon – don't miss it!

From Cardiff, take the M4 again, west to Swansea on the frontier between the industrial sprawl of South Wales and the beauty of the west. Swansea is the second city of Wales, a keen rival to Cardiff in everything including the national religion – rugby. It has no pub to match the Golden Cross' Victorian splendours, but the Adam & Eve provides as warm a pub welcome as any.

The Adam & Eve poses me a problem, for it will have been renovated between my visit and the publication of this book, and, as we have seen in many pubs around Britain, renovations are by no means always carried out in a manner sympathetic to a pub's character. I am taking a chance that the Adam & Eve renovations will not spoil the flavour of the pub, but the Pearces have run the pub for many years, and it is fair to assume that they know their business and will tolerate no 'improvements' which prove to be the opposite.

The Adam & Eve was a wine store of that name in the 1800s, and during the renovations, many old bottles were unearthed. More recently

The Adam & Eve
Licensees: Mr & Mrs Pearce
207 High Street,
Swansea,
West Glamorgan
☎ Swansea (0792) 55913
11.30 - 3.30; 5.30 - 10.30
(11 Friday & Saturday)

Brain Dark, Bitter, SA

Lunchtime food. Garden.

*The Adam & Eve, Swansea –
Dylan Thomas drank here*

it was a haunt of Swansea's most celebrated son, Dylan Thomas, almost as famed for his drinking exploits as for his poetry and prose. Thomas would no longer recognise the pub interior, but I think he would still feel at home there, and he might well recognise the licensees, who have been in charge since 1950.

The other great attraction in the area is the Gower, Swansea's private peninsula to the west, which has a host of prehistoric sites set in some spectacular scenery. There is a neolithic burial chamber, Park Cwm, at Penmaen, the Paviland Caves near Port Eynon and Arthur's Stone, a megalithic tomb, near Reynoldston. As the name suggests, the twenty-five ton covering stone is linked by legend with King Arthur. There are also the ruins of Penrice Castle and, at The Mumbles, those of the spectacularly sited Oystermouth Castle.

Once more, the dilettantes now have the chance to take a break from the classic town pubs trek and disappear into west Wales. You can pursue the Dylan Thomas connection to Laugharne in Dyfed, where he lived for several years and is buried, or follow the coasts and mountains west and north. The landscape is constantly punctuated by the ruins of castles, mute testimony to the difficulties which the English kings had in imposing their rule on their unwilling Welsh subjects. The next part of our classic town pubs journey, however, takes us through country with an even more troubled history, the Welsh Marches, marked by the eighth-century Offa's Dyke and by another chain of castles and fortified towns.

The handsome frontage of the Punch House, Monmouth, is more than matched by its welcoming interior

We begin at Monmouth, at the junction of the River Monnow with the Wye, the site of the Roman Blestium and the strategic key to the whole of South Wales. In addition to Monmouth's eleventh-century castle, where Henry V was born, there is the fortified town gate on the bridge over the Monnow, which is unique in Britain, and a marvellous pub, the Punch House.

The Punch House stands on Agincourt Square, named after the famous victory of one of its famous sons, Henry V. A bronze statue in the Square commemorates another, more recent one, Charles Rolls, one half of the Rolls Royce partnership.

The Punch House is a stately black and white building, dating from the seventeenth century. In summer it is almost submerged in an avalanche of flowers from its window boxes and hanging baskets, and in 1987 the pub won the Wales in Bloom competition. On fine days you can sit outside at tables on the cobbles and admire the flowers while you take a drink.

The Punch theme is reflected in reliefs of the Punch figure on the walls, the picture of the pub dog, a spaniel called Punch, on the sign, and in bound copies of the original issues of the eponymous magazine in a case by the door. The pub needs no gimmicks, however, for it is an absolute beauty. The interior is full of character, with a huge fireplace, oak beams, much copper and brass, and the old oak gate from the town gaol. At the far end of the bar is a food servery and you can also eat in the beautiful upstairs restaurant, sitting at one of several fine antique tables. One table, at which Lord Nelson and Lady Hamilton once ate, will accommodate as many as sixteen people.

The food is quite superb, as outstanding as the pub and the beer. You can eat fresh Wye salmon and a host of good dishes, and everything is freshly made from local ingredients. The pub also butchers its own meat, smokes its own fish and ham and cures its own bacon. The restaurant is a welcome addition to the range of good reasons for visiting this excellent pub, but it does not dominate what in any case is as comfortable and characterful a pub as you will find in many a mile.

From Monmouth the A466 runs due north to Hereford, scene of a grim siege in the Civil War, described by Defoe: 'Tis a large and populous city, and in the time of the late Rebellion, was very strong, and being well fortified, and as well defended, supported a tedious and very severe siege; for besides the Parliament's forces, who could never reduce it, the Scots army was called to the work, who lay before it, 'till they laid above 4000 of their bones there, and at last, it was rather taken by the fate of the war, than by the attacks of the besiegers.'

The road joins with the A49 and crosses Ridge Hill just south of Hereford, which gives fine views towards the city. The Hereford skyline is dominated by the cathedral,

The Punch House
Licensee: John Wills
Agincourt Square, Monmouth
☎ Monmouth (0600) 3855
11.30 - 3 (4 Friday, Saturday & Monday); 6 - 11

Draught Bass; Wadworth 6X; Worthington Best Bitter

Lunchtime & evening food. Restaurant. Outside drinking area.

The lovely setting of the Saracens Head, Hereford

built, according to legend, because an apparition of St Ethelbert, who was murdered by King Offa of Mercia in 794, demanded that a church be built on the spot to atone for his murder. The church was built over the tomb of St Ethelbert in 825; it has been much rebuilt in the succeeding centuries, but is a dramatic sight, particularly at night when it is floodlit. The cathedral also houses two priceless treasures, the huge Mappa Mundi of Richard of Haldingham dating from around 1275, and the chained library, the largest in the world; 1500 manuscripts and early printed books are chained to a shelf so that they can be read, but not removed. The shelf dates from the early seventeenth century, some of the books date from the fifteenth century.

The best view of the cathedral is to be had from outside the Saracens Head, which stands on the banks of the Wye on the site of the old city gates, once the boundary between England and Wales. Get yourself a drink and enjoy the view across the Wye, drifting slowly by below you.

Like the Adam & Eve in Swansea, the Saracens Head was undergoing alterations at the time of my visit; again I am trusting that the new, improved Saracens Head is a classic pub, and one worthy of its beautiful site. One half of the pub is now devoted to the food trade, but the atmosphere in the riverside bar remains unmistakably that of a pub. There is an alcove to one side with a dartboard, and in addition to its darts team, the pub runs two cricket teams and has a skittles alley. Have a last look at the cathedral

The Saracens Head Inn
Licensees: Desmond & Pauline Davies
1, 3 & 5 St Martins Street, Hereford
☎ Hereford (0432) 275480
11 - 2.30; 6 - 11

Draught Bass; Courage Directors Bitter; Hereford Bitter; Marston Pedigree; Guest Beers

Lunchtime & evening food. Riverside patio.

over the river, then head north towards Ludlow.

Unlike most of its border neighbours, Ludlow was never destroyed by the Welsh or English and it survives as a delightful town, full of fine buildings. The exterior of the Feathers is world famous; sadly the interior is an object lesson in how to spoil an old and characterful pub interior. Try the Bull, the Wheatsheaf or the Church instead, or have a look at the eleventh-century castle, which was occupied in the fourteenth century by Roger Mortimer, the lover of Queen Isabella; together they murdered her husband, Edward II. It was also the site of the death of Prince Arthur, whose heart was buried in St Lawrence's church. His younger brother, Henry VIII, inherited both his throne and his wife, Catherine of Aragon. When you have seen enough of Ludlow, carry on to Shrewsbury to the next classic pub.

The Boathouse, Shrewsbury – once a storehouse for bodies, now an excellent pub

Shrewsbury stands in a meander of the river Severn, and has been a settlement since the fifth century. Offa captured it in the eighth century, and in 1138, the Norman Stephan de Blois seized the castle and hanged the whole castle garrison. His bloody traditions were maintained by Edward I, who ruled from it during his campaigns against the Welsh and hanged David, the last king of Wales, there in 1283. Charles I made the town his headquarters in 1642, but three years later it fell to the Parliamentary army.

Take the road out of Shrewsbury towards Welshpool, cross the river and then turn left onto the A488 towards Bishops Castle. The Boat House is on the left-hand side a few hundred yards along on the banks of the Severn. It is a half-timbered building, dating back to the fifteenth century. There are three rooms inside, all looking out over the river. The pub has beams, bare boards, oak pillars, dark panelling and a fine carved fireplace with a blazing open fire in winter. The walls are decorated with oars and various bits of nautical and even ocean-going memorabilia and everything has a rich patina of age (or is it nicotine?).

In summer, the bars are open onto the terrace and rose garden by the riverside, a lovely place to enjoy a drink. There are barbecues when the weather allows, and you can cross the river by a footbridge and wander through Quarry Park, back towards Shrewsbury. The cellars below the pub, now used for storing beer, had a more grisly function at the time of the plague. They were used as a charnel house, storing the corpses of Shrewsbury's hundreds of plague deaths.

If that thought has not put you off pubs for the time being, drive on north towards Chester,

The Boathouse Inn
Licensee: Brian Branagh
New Street
Porthill,
Shrewsbury,
☎ Shrewsbury (0743) 62965
11 - 3; 6 - 11

EST? 1742

Flowers Original, IPA

Lunchtime food. Families welcome. Riverside garden & terrace.

Opposite: The Olde Custom House, Chester – a pub as full of character as the great city in which it stands

a great Roman settlement and the most beautifully preserved medieval town in Britain.

Chester – Castra Devana – was the headquarters of the Roman twentieth legion and its importance is shown by the size of its excavated amphitheatre, the largest Roman building in Britain so far discovered, capable of accommodating 9000 spectators. The medieval walls encircle the old city, following the line of the Roman fortifications to the north and east of the city and varying in height up to thirty-three feet.

The old city contains some stunning half-timbered buildings and the unique Rows, a tremendous attraction to tourists today, though Defoe was rather less impressed on his visit in the 1720s: 'It is a very ancient city, and to this day, the buildings are very old; nor do the Rows as they call them, add anything, in my opinion, to the beauty of the city; but just the contrary, they serve to make the city look both old and ugly. These Rows are certain long galleries, up one pair of stairs, which run along the side of the streets, before all the houses, though joined to them, and as is pretended, they are to keep the people dry in walking along. This they do indeed effectually, but then they take away all the view of the houses from the streets, nor can a stranger, that was to ride through Chester see any shops in the city; besides, they make the shops themselves dark, and the way in them is dark, dirty and uneven.' Judge for yourself, there are two classic pubs to try, both in the heart of the old city.

The Falcon has a beautiful half-timbered façade, with massive beams supporting the first floor jutting out over the street. The pub was derelict in the early 1980s, but has been lovingly restored. Step off the street past the massive stone blocks of the entrance arch, into a bar with huge oak beams and pillars, two fireplaces and a food servery. Through an arch is another room with a huge fireplace, and down a couple of steps is a third area.

The wattle-and-daub construction of the walls has been exposed and preserved in one or two places, both in the downstairs bar and in the upstairs function room, which was the original fifteenth-century living quarters of the Duke of Westminster, who had the place as a town house. Now it is used for live music: trad jazz every Thursday night and Saturday lunchtime, folk music on Wednesday evening.

The beer cellar is housed in a twelfth-century crypt, and when the pub is not too busy, the Walkers are usually happy to show people round. The beams in the cellars were taken from old sailing ships and are massive pieces of oak.

The Falcon
Licensees: Andrew & Gail Walker
Lower Bridge Street, Chester
☎ Chester (0244) 42060
11 - 3; 5.30 - 11

Samuel Smith Old Brewery Bitter; Museum Ale

Lunchtime food. Function room.

The fine half-timbering of the Falcon, Chester

The Falcon has two ghosts, one in the cellar and one upstairs, which is alleged to walk through the wall from the building next door.

Cross the road from the Falcon and go up Bridge Street, past some more magnificent half-timbered buildings. At first floor level are Chester's famous Rows, where you may wish to lose yourself for an hour or two. Carry on up the street and turn left into Watergate Street at the top, by the Market Cross. Halfway down is another quite superb half-timbered building, Bishop Lloyd's Palace, and further down on the left is Chester's other classic pub, the Olde Custome House.

The pub takes it name from the old custom house across the road and is another fine half-timbered building, once known as the Star Inn. It was restored in 1637 by Thomas Weaver, whose initials and the year still appear on the gable outside, and it may then have been a haberdasher's rather than an inn. Though the building is a venerable one, the pub is as warm and friendly as the most homespun local.

Step into the large bar, with a fine, carved fireplace complete with log stove and bench seats right around the room. There is a dartboard and a prodigious collection of trophies in a cupboard alongside it, which suggests it may be wiser not to play the regulars for money! At one end is a low-ceilinged parlour area. At the back is a lounge with a pine fireplace, old benches, china jugs and gleaming copper and brass. At lunchtime it acts as the dining-room, the home-made food usually including a roast, but in the evening it reverts to being a lounge. From there you can step through into the Hall Bar, which has a fireplace with carved oak panels inset.

On the wall is an old in-going document dating from 1824, which lists a few of the obligations of an early nineteenth-century landlord: it cost Joseph Walker £20 to take over the running of the pub and he had to undertake not to 'fraudulently dilute or adulterate the Beer, Ale and other Liquors ... not knowingly suffer gaming or any other sedentary game ... No Men or Women of notoriously bad fame or dissolute Girls and Boys ... No Drinking or Tippling during the hours of Divine Service ... No Bull, Bear or Badger baiting or Cock fighting.'

While the whole of the Welsh border area is rich in fine half-timbered buildings, Chester houses a particularly remarkable concentration of them, making it a most appropriate place to end this part of the journey round our classic town pubs. The next stage takes us to an area equally as rich in history, fine buildings and superb pubs.

Ye Olde Custome House
Licensee: Ken Gander
Watergate Street,
Chester
☎ Chester (0244) 24435
11.30 - 3; 5.30 - 11

Marston Border Mild, Bitter, Exhibition; Marston Pedigree

Lunchtime food.

OXFORD,
THE FOREST OF ARDEN
& THE FOREST OF DEAN

The next part of the classic pubs journey travels through some of our oldest and most historic cities before ending in an area which was the first to feel the dawning of the industrial age in Britain. The first stop is at Oxford, described by Defoe as 'a noble flourishing city, so possessed of all that can contribute to make the residence of the scholars easy and comfortable, that no spot of ground in England goes beyond it.'

Trying to convey something of the flavour of Oxford in a few lines is a virtual impossibility. The Sheldonian, the Radcliffe Camera, Christ Church, Magdalen with its deer park and the tower from where choirs sing on May Morning, are a start; for the rest, follow where your footsteps and your curiosity lead you, or buy a guide book. You are in one of the world's great university cities; take your time!

The Bear, Oxford – many pubs showed their allegiance to kings or nobles by displaying their emblems, in this case, the bear and ragged staff

The Bear is just a few yards from Carfax, the focus of the city, but sheltered from its noise down narrow, high-walled lanes. Reach it from either Alfred Street, off the High Street (locally known as 'the High'), or from Blue Boar Street, off St Aldates. There are window boxes and hanging baskets of flowers in summer and a carved wooden sign of a bear and ragged staff.

There has been an inn on or near the site of the Bear since 1242. The present building was originally the stables and accommodation for the stable lads, when the inn was a coaching inn. Before that, the site had been used as a burial ground; human bones were found in the cellar as recently as ten years ago. Given that history, it is perhaps not surprising that the pub is haunted.

The Bear is also traditionally the haunt of students from the nearby Christchurch and Oriel Colleges and is no place for the faint-hearted when celebrations of 'Eights Week', May Morning or the end of 'Schools' (final examinations to the rest of us), are in full flow. On May Morning the celebrations begin early; many pubs open from 6.30am to 8am, dispensing Buck's Fizz and other delights to the early risers.

What distinguishes The Bear most of all, though, is its monstrous collection of ties. There are over 7000 tie-ends snipped from willing and occasionally unwilling donors and new samples are constantly arriving from all over the world. The glass cases in which they are housed now spread across the ceiling of one of the pub's small connecting rooms, as well as all around the walls.

Previous page: Part of the prodigious collection of ties at the Bear, Oxford

There is an open fire, wood panelling and bench seats, and the oak beams and ceilings are

The Bear
Licensees: Mr & Mrs M.L. Rusling
Alfred Street,
Oxford
☎ Oxford (0865) 244680
11 - 2.30; 5.30 - 11

Halls Harvest Bitter; Ind Coope Burton Ale

Lunchtime & evening food (until 8.30). Families welcome. Outside drinking area.

rich in that unique pub patina of age mixed with tobacco smoke. Outside, you can sit at wooden benches on a terrace just off the lane, where you can watch the world go by and listen to the bell of Great Tom just over the wall in Christchurch. Every night at five past nine, it rings 101 times to commemorate the college founders.

The other obligatory stop around the city is the thirteenth-century Turf Tavern, in a passage off Swan Place, leading off Holywell Street, behind Hartford College. The Turf features in Thomas Hardy's *Jude the Obscure* and is probably Oxford's most famous pub. It is also among its most expensive; the Turf's tiny bar must take more money per square foot than anywhere else in England! There are four outside drinking areas beneath enormous umbrellas and, in springtime, showers of cherry blossom. These areas are always packed in summer. If the aroma of cooking gets too much to bear, let me lead you to some very different classic pubs.

After the peace and tranquility of pubs that are centuries-old, you may be in the mood for something brash, lively and noisy by way of a contrast. If so, look no further than the Oxford Bakery & Brewhouse by Gloucester Green. It spent many years as the Old Red Lion and was by no means the most exciting pub in Gloucester Green, never mind Oxford. Then came the transformation; it was pulled inside out and upside down and emerged as a warren of rough-hewn drinking areas on several different levels, all with at least a nodding acquaintance with the large central bar.

There are stone flags, old brick, rough pine, hop sacks and dried flowers and, even if the pub is as near brand new as makes no difference, it has been designed with good pub principles in mind and is a pleasure to drink in as a result . . . but do not call in if you are looking for a quiet spot for a ruminative pint and a ponder on the meaning of life.

As the name suggests, the Brewhouse produces its own beers on the premises, though CAMRA purists object to them being stored under a blanket of CO_2. However, for those who can't bring themselves to try the home-brewed range, there are always guest bars on tap as well as exotic imported Belgian beers such as Chimay, Duvel, Kriek and Framboise. To accompany the pub's own beer, try some of the bread baked in the adjoining bakery. You can fill your 'Trencher' with English regional cheeses, salt beef, cold cuts and salads, and on weekday evenings there is a gargantuan deep-pan pizza with garlic bread that provides a filling, if somewhat anti-social snack. If you are there on May Morning you can try a bacon trencher, kippers

Oxford Bakery & Brewhouse
Licensee: Charles Cassidy
14 Gloucester Street, Oxford
☎ Oxford (0865) 727265
10.30 - 2.30; 5.30 - 11

Oxford Brewhouse Tapper, Best, Porter, Oxbow; Guest beers

Lunchtime & evening food. Families welcome. Garden.

One of Oxford's most popular forms of transport, outside one of Oxford's most popular pubs – the Oxford Brewery & Bakehouse

or scrambled eggs to help the Buck's Fizz or Black Velvet down; there may even be oysters too.

If you haven't drunk your fill by closing time, you can take two or five gallon packs of the house beers away with you and during the day you can watch your beer being brewed through a series of glass windows at the back of the pub. Outside is a garden with an unhappy-looking tree and a large Escheresque mural. On Wednesday evenings and Sunday lunchtimes there is live music covering the full gamut of jazz; at other times the Brewhouse plays jazz selections from its huge collection of tapes. The Brewhouse is always busy and often very noisy; you will not find Old Bert in a corner playing dominoes, but you will find a lot of people having the time of their lives.

If you like live music then the Radcliffe Arms Tavern in Cranham Street, off Walton Street in Jericho, is the place for you. Every night of the week a musician or band squeezes onto the tiny stage and lets you have it right between the ears. Again, it is not a place to take your aged relatives, but it is a great place for a lively night out.

Having sampled the delights of Oxford city centre, there are two pubs on the outskirts which are musts. All Oxford students will have happy memories of lazy summer days by the river; visit the Perch and the Trout and you will be able to share a little of the magic.

The ideal way to arrive at the Perch is by punt. On foot, you can either walk out across

The Perch, Binsey – a beautiful pub in a lovely setting

Port Meadow and across the footbridge over the river or go out past the station on Botley Road and stroll along the river bank. If you really cannot be persuaded to stretch your legs, drive out past the station and turn right onto Binsey Lane. Follow it for the couple of miles that take you to the tiny hamlet of Binsey. You will find the Perch down by the river.

Often the promise of a beautiful, thatched pub in a stunning setting is shattered as you step through its doors, but the Perch is every bit as good inside as out, and the warmth of the welcome matches the quality of the pub. It burned down ten years ago, but has been so well restored that you would have to look very hard to see the joins.

The beamed and stone-flagged bar has log stoves at either end and a food servery off to one side, with a room where families can sit. A conservatory leads to a beautiful (and award-winning) lawned garden stretching down to the river. There are wooden benches under the willows and a very well-equipped children's play area. Lewis Carroll is said to have made the first reading of his *Alice in Wonderland* stories to some friends in the garden of the Perch; he will crop up again when we reach the last of our Oxford classic pubs.

The Perch is first documented in the fifteenth century, but is certainly much older, and it was much used by pilgrims on their way to the nearby Church of St Mary in Binsey, which had a well credited with healing powers. The well is still in existence, though you may find the healing powers of an hour or two at the Perch just as beneficial. Its riverside setting perhaps explains the ghost of a sailor which has been seen in the pub cellar.

The food at the Perch is as excellent and traditional as the pub itself. All the dishes are home-made and celebrate the regional cuisine of Britain. Wiltshire Chicken, Kentish Beef, Somerset Pork or Binsey-style Trout will please your palate without emptying your wallet. The food at the next classic pub is excellent too; perhaps you should walk off your lunch along the riverbank so that you can find room for dinner at the Trout at Godstow.

To reach the Trout by road, drive north out of Oxford along the Woodstock Road; the best time to do so is in spring, when the trees lining the road are in blossom. Take the turn down to Wolvercote off the roundabout and drive through the village and up to the Trout.

As you step through the gate down onto the stone terrace you may hear the distinctive cry of a peacock. The pub has several, and in their

The Perch
Licensees: Vaughan & Sue Jagger
Binsey Lane,
Binsey,
Oxford
☎ Oxford (0865) 240386
11 - 2.30; 5.30 - 11

Arkell BBB; Halls Harvest Bitter; Ind Coope Burton Ale

Lunchtime & evening food. Families welcome. Garden. Mooring facilities.

*The Trout, Lower Wolvercote –
part of every Oxford student's
memories*

summer plumage they make fitting jewels in the
Trout's lovely setting. A weir cascades down,
the river is full of leaping fish, which you can
hand-feed (mostly chub, despite the pub
name!), and from the end of the terrace is a
quite stunning view of the distant Oxford skyline. Across a rustic bridge over the river is a
two-and-a-half acre island, which has a Victorian garden with arbours, stone statues and a
sun dial. There is also an Italian sunken garden
and even a World War II Anderson shelter! On
the terrace outside the Trout there is a bar
which dispenses soft drinks and Pimms (but of
course, this is Oxford . . .) on fine days.

Inside the Trout is a stone-flagged bar, with
gleaming pewter and an old spit roaster, driven
by a clock mechanism, above a huge stone fireplace. Off to one side is a small parlour with oak
seats and a stone fireplace, at the other end is an
oak-beamed restaurant with a carved Jacobean
bedstead behind the bar. You can eat at the bar
or from the à la carte menu with, perhaps inevitably, a stuffed trout speciality.

Like the Perch up the river, the Trout is
steeped in historic associations. Lewis Carroll
figures in the Trout's story too; he used to bring
the real-life Alice here, take her punting and tell
her his stories. In the seventeenth century the
pub was a brothel for the university, but its most
interesting piece of alleged history comes much
earlier.

The Trout was built in the twelfth century
and was used by Henry II. While he was away
on his adventures, his mistress, the Fair Rosamund, remained in the nunnery just across the

The Trout
*Licensees: Gianni & Gill
Cozzolino*
95 Godstow Road,
Lower Wolvercote,
Oxford
☎ (0865) 54485
11 - 2.30; 6 - 11

Draught Bass; Charrington
IPA

Lunchtime & evening food.
Restaurant. Riverside
terrace.

fields from the Trout. When he returned, he would wave a lamp from the window and Rosamund would travel through a tunnel (which comes up behind the present bar in the restaurant) to spend the night with her lover.

The Queen, Eleanor of Aquitaine, discovered this arrangement and lured Rosamund across to the Trout by waving a lantern from the upstairs window. When Rosamund came out of the tunnel, she was seized by the Queen's men at arms, and taken upstairs to be killed. She was offered the choice of poison or the knife, and took poison. Even in death she was not allowed to rest in peace, her body was dug up from its grave and thrown onto the riverbank. Rosamund's ghost is said to walk the upper rooms and the garden of the Trout. She has been seen in the bedroom, visible only from the knees up, for her ghost is walking the original floor, two feet below the present level. On the anniversary of her death the counterpane of the bed in the room where she died is said to be pulled from the bed.

Rosamund's ring, now in the Ashmolean, was found on the island in the river outside the Trout; her headstone, much weathered, is set in the wall just before you reach Wolvercote, a few yards down the road from a memorial to two Royal Flying Corps airmen who met their deaths in a monoplane crash on 10 September 1912.

A later Henry also played a part in the history of the Trout, for it was destroyed at the time of Henry VIII's dissolution of the monasteries, though it was rebuilt soon after. Most of the building dates from the sixteenth century, though the floors, the two fireplaces and the Stable Bar are original.

We will shortly be making for Stratford upon Avon, a tourist attraction to rival Oxford itself, but first we will call at Warwick, already a great town in the fourteenth and fifteenth centuries, when Stratford was nothing more than a market town in the Forest of Arden. The fourteenth-century castle sits on a crag high above the Avon, built on the site of fortifications which go back as far as the early years of the tenth century. The twelfth-century church of St Mary was almost entirely rebuilt after the Fire of Warwick, which virtually destroyed the whole town in 1694. In the north wall of the chapel is the tomb of Robert Dudley, Earl of Leicester, whose wife died in mysterious and highly convenient circumstances at a time when he was rumoured to be the lover of Elizabeth I.

In a quiet street in the shadow of the church tower, you will find the peaceful oasis of the Zetland Arms, a fifteenth-century pub, also re-

The Zetland Arms
Licensee: Mrs Rita North
Church Street,
Warwick
Warwickshire
☎ Warwick (0926) 491974
10.30 - 2.30; 5.30 - 11

Davenports Traditional Bitter

Lunchtime food. Evening food: sandwiches and rolls only. Families welcome at lunchtime. Garden. Accommodation.

built after the Fire of Warwick.

Inside the pub there is a small wood-panelled bar leading off the hall and a larger bar with a stone fireplace at the back. This latter room opens onto the Zetland Arms' finest feature, a delightful, award-winning, walled garden. It is a beautiful, peaceful place to sit and on a hot summer day there can be few more pleasant places to enjoy a cooling drink than under the trees surrounded by walls smothered in honeysuckle, savouring the scents of a mass of sweet-smelling flowers.

When you are relaxed and refreshed, travel on to Stratford, where in summer at least, the atmosphere is anything but relaxed.

Shakespearian spoken here – the Dirty Duck, Stratford on Avon

S ratford on Avon is Britain's number one tourist town after London, with enough tourists threading their way in and out of the half-timbering every day to people the casts of the complete works of Shakespeare several times over. The effects of this flood are all-pervasive, but there are several pubs that have avoided the worst of the kitsch tourist treatment meted out by architects and designers elsewhere. Mercifully, no-one has yet had the idea of a Shakespeare theme park, but it cannot be long delayed!

Perhaps the two best-known pubs are the two Swans – the White Swan and the Black Swan, whose nickname, 'the Dirty Duck', has now become its official name. If you want to spend the day rubber-necking in search of famous Shakespearian actors, the Dirty Duck is the place for you. Overlooking the River Avon, it is close to the Memorial Theatre, and caters extensively for the theatre trade, with pre- and post-performance meals. The Long Bar is lined with signed photographs of famous actors and actresses. There is a paved terrace looking out over the riverside gardens and a venerable mulberry bush growing out of the wall of the pub. The Dirty Duck is on most visitors' calling list; for that reason it is absolutely packed-out in the tourist season, and I prefer the less frenzied atmosphere at another Stratford pub.

The Dirty Duck (formerly The Black Swan)
Manager: Pamela J Harris
Waterside,
Stratford on Avon,
Warwickshire
☎ Stratford on Avon (0789) 297312
10.30 - 2.30; 5.30 - 11

EST.ᴰ 1742

Flowers IPA, Original

Lunchtime & evening food. Restaurant (closed Sunday). Families only on the terrace.

Opposite: Pub and church, the twin pillars of British social life down the centuries – the Zetland Arms, Warwick

The White Swan looks out onto the Market Square. The market, held every Friday, dates from 1196; the White Swan is not quite that old, but it is the oldest building in Stratford used as an inn. It dates from the early fifteenth century and was built originally as the house of a prosperous family. It is now a three star hotel, but still retains many fine original features. The handsome half-timbered frontage is decorated with flower tubs and hanging baskets in summer, and there are leaded windows with stained glass panels inset in them, and lead drainpipes decorated with swan emblems, fleur de lys, scallop shells and white roses.

Inside is a wealth of oak panelling and furniture. In the entrance hall is a grandfather clock with a man in the moon rolling his eyes as it ticks. One of the first floor bedrooms is the ancient Solar, where the master of the house slept. There is a fine king post roof and a tiny stone window that once looked out on the Forest of Arden . . . now it looks out on a forest of rooftops.

The jewel of the White Swan is the Oak Room, once the bar parlour of the old inn, with superb, carved oak furniture and panelling, massive oak beams and a remarkable medieval wall-painting of Tobit and the Angel, which was uncovered during renovation work in 1927.

Off the Oak Room is the one part of the White Swan that really justifies the term 'pub': the Good Companions Bar, with a big open fireplace and a really relaxing atmosphere. After a hard day trudging round the sights of Stratford, what better way to unwind than over a pint in the peace and calm of this ancient inn? When you have recovered from the rigours of the day, you can eat in the restaurant, which, in keeping with its surroundings, specializes in good English food from good English ingredients.

Visit, if you can stand the crowds, Shakespeare's birthplace, Anne Hathaway's cottage and Shakespeare's last resting place, the fine thirteenth-century Holy Trinity Church. No name appears on his grave in the channel of the church, just the inscription, claimed to have been written by Shakespeare himself:
'Good friend, for Jesus' sake forebear
To dig the dust enclosed here.
Blest be the man that spares these stones,
And curst be he that moves my bones.'
When you have seen enough of Stratford, head west to Worcester.

Take the A422 from Stratford which skirts the Vale of Evesham on its way down to Worcester. When people talk about Olde Englande this is probably the sort of landscape they have in mind: half-timbered, thatch-

The White Swan
Manager: David Warnes
Rother Street,
Stratford upon Avon,
Warwickshire
10.30 - 2.30; 5.30 - 11

Marston Pedigree;
Wadworth 6X; Webster
Yorkshire Bitter

Lunchtime & evening food.
Restaurant.
Accommodation. Families
welcome.

ed buildings and a soft, rolling countryside without hard edges – a perfect setting for some mythic golden age.

The Vale has many similarities to the Garden of England in Kent, in particular a climate that is soft enough for fruit and hop growing to be equally dominant. Here you are also on the first fringes of cider country, which runs from Hereford and Worcester down through Gloucester to the Somerset and Devon cider heartlands.

As you approach Worcester, the spires of the cathedral come into view. Abandon your car in one of the car parks close to the cathedral and explore the city on foot; both of Worcester's classic pubs are only a gentle stroll from the cathedral.

Worcester has as bloody a history as most ancient English cities. Saxons, Danes and Welsh laid it waste, and Cromwell's Roundhead troops laid siege to it and plundered it after driving out Charles II. The Commandery, founded by St Wulfstan in 1085, became the Royalist headquarters at the Battle of Worcester and is preserved as a Civil War Centre. Pilgrims to the tomb of St Wulfstan provided the money with which the cathedral was extended from the early twelfth century onwards. The massive fourteenth-century tower juts defiantly above the Severn.

The Cardinal's Hat is close to the cathedral though its immediate outlook is dominated by the spiralling concrete ramp of a multi-storey car park. If nothing else, it guarantees you can park near the pub, and, once in-

The Cardinal's Hat
Licensees: Mavis & Fred Wells
Friar Street,
Worcester
☎ Worcester (0905) 21890
12 - 2.30; 7 - 11

Davenports Bitter

Families welcome.
Lunchtime sandwiches, no evening food.

The Cardinal's Hat, Worcester – no lampreys, no brawls!

side, you can forget about concrete and the internal combustion engine and relax in a pub that is old and full of history, yet remains refreshingly down-to-earth.

An oak-panelled passageway leads to the back bar with its fine stone fireplace, rather spoiled by its gas fire and copperette surround. There is panelling and some fine carved oak furniture, but better than this is the front bar, where there are beams garlanded with hops, some half-timbering and the emblem of the cardinal's hat over another stone fireplace. Here you can have a quiet drink in a corner or join in the chat across the bar.

The Sealed Knot, that society of masochists dedicated to re-creating the battles of the Civil War, hold their meetings in the room across the hall. On the wall of the bar is a damaged helmet from one of their battles, testifying to Pikeman John's good fortune in losing no more than his hair and part of his helmet when a gun went off behind him.

The pub was first mentioned in 1518, when the New Year gifts to Prior Moore of Worcester Cathedral included 'gift of Mococke of ye Cardinall's Hat, a lampfrey', and it also features in the papers of Henry VIII in connection with a brawl that took place at the inn. You are unlikely to find either brawls or lampfreys on the menu today; the Cardinal's Hat serves virtually no food, only rolls at lunchtime. There are no chips, no machines and no gimmicks, and it is just a timeless epitome of a fine town local.

If you are looking for food or a livelier atmosphere, step along the city walls to Lowesmoor and a very different, but equally excellent pub – the Jolly Roger Brewery Tap. The brewery moved to Worcester from Upton on Severn in 1985 and, after many wrangles with the licensing magistrates, Paul Soden succeeded in obtaining a licence that enabled him to open the Brewery Tap as a pub. The building was carefully de-modernised, with genuine Yorkshire flagstones and floorboards, old brick and beams, and barrels for tables; it is a tribute to the care with which the work was done that the Jolly Roger has all the atmosphere and character of a pub that has been in its present form for centuries rather than a few years.

At the back of the pub is the brewery, which can be seen through the windows; they brew three times a week so there is about an even chance that you can watch the brewer at work. Nearby is a small snug with a fine elm table, where you can enjoy a quiet drink. The hop-garlanded main bar is lively and can be boisterous on Friday and Saturday nights, when you can hear live jazz or blues, sometimes by the

The beer that keeps the Jolly Roger flying – the Jolly Roger Brewery Tap, Worcester

The Jolly Roger Brewery Tap
Licensee: Paul Soden
50 Lowesmoor,
Worcester
☎ Worcester (0905) 21540

Quaff Ale, Three Counties Best Bitter, Severn Bore Special, Old Lowesmoor, Worcester Winter Wobbler, regular special brews

Lunchtime & evening food. Families welcome. Brewery tours by arrangement.

pub's own Jolly Roger Blues Band. During the rest of the week, the pub is quieter, with live music confined to the gentler strains of folk.

Off the main bar is an extremely good value food servery, with local produce ranging from an excellent cold table, through Desperate Dan burgers to a three pound T-bone steak, though you have to give them 48-hours notice if you want to attempt this ultimate challenge. If you are in a hurry, you can phone your order ahead.

The Jolly Roger hosts a remarkable variety of events and activities including a Quaffers' Association, which raises money for charity while members involve themselves in ridiculous pursuits. There is also a splendid variant on the annual Beaujolais Nouveau race (which sees teams from many of Britain's independent brewers racing across to Rouen), where Frenchmen are introduced to the delights of such brews as the Jolly Roger's Winter Wobbler, before the participants return to England with the first of the new season's Beaujolais Nouveau.

The licensee, Paul Soden, is also chairman of the Small Independent Brewers Association, whose members contribute so much to the character, diversity and quality of British pubs and the beers we drink in them. His brewery and his pub are a fair measure of what independent local brewers can still offer in this multinational age, and the Jolly Roger Brewery Tap demonstrates that pubs do not have to stand still to succeed or be valued. They have always changed and always will, but that change must be in keeping with the values that have made our pubs unique, not in accord with some mid-

There is as warm a welcome as you could wish at the Jolly Roger Brewery Tap, Worcester

Atlantic man's fantasies that will end by replacing our pubs with soulless, American-style bars.

You can take the motorway down from Worcester to Tewkesbury, but the A38 is a much more pleasant route. Once nose-to-tail with grumpy holidaymakers on their way down to the West Country, the A38 is now mercifully peaceful, as all the holiday traffic sits immobile on the M5 instead. To your right are the Malvern Hills; Elgar buffs should turn up the Cello Concerto or the Enigma Variations to full volume and spend an hour or so wandering the hills. Those with tin ears or raging thirsts will continue straight on to Tewkesbury.

Ye Olde Black Bear stands guard at the entrance to Tewkesbury, just by the bridge over the Mill Avon, which links the Avon with the Severn. The pub looks beautiful from the outside and its promise is amply fulfilled once you step inside. It dates from the twelfth century, though the present half-timbered structure is sixteenth century. Its sign of a bear and ragged staff belongs to the crest of the Beauchamp family and was adopted for the pub by one of their retainers. The bear on the sign was 'fed' with hot cross buns every Easter in a custom that lasted until wartime rationing killed it off.

The Bear exudes the character and atmosphere you would expect in an inn of its great age and it is crammed full of interesting features. The lounge bar was once the stabling for the inn. It was built in 1422 when the charge for stabling was three horses for a penny a day. Horseshoes on display in the bar were found in the area. The massive oak beams, etched windows and open fireplace all add to the character of this room, which was used as a field hospital during the Battle of Tewkesbury in 1481, the decisive battle of the Wars of the Roses.

A long corridor links the lounge bar with the other rooms; in one there is a pool table, and in another, the family room, you are likely to make the acquaintance of the pub ghost, an old lady who occupies a corner seat. The wall which divides the family room from the public bar is the oldest part of the building, and is fifteen feet thick, leaving room for a cupboard and a staircase inside it; perhaps there is also a priest hole waiting to be discovered.

If the rest of the pub is distinctive, the public bar is unique. The decorated ceiling is leather and was made by Italian craftsmen who lodged at the inn while working on the Abbey. The story is that they did the pub ceiling in return for free beer and accommodation. The carved wooden bar is claimed to have been made from the Abbey choir stalls, which were removed from the Abbey at the time of Henry VIII's dis-

Ye Olde Black Bear
Licensees: Dave & Cheryl Webb
High Street,
Tewkesbury,
Gloucestershire
☎ Tewkesbury (0684) 292202
11 - 2.30; 6 - 11

EST.ᴰ 1742

Flowers IPA, Original

Lunchtime & evening food. Families welcome. Children's menu. Riverside garden. Moorings available. Afternoon teas & barbecues at weekends and bank holidays.

solution of the monasteries.

Outside is a terraced garden, leading down to the river. If you have arrived by car, you can relax on the lawns and watch the traffic on the river. If you are travelling by boat, moor it at the Bear's landing stage and enjoy a break in one of the most characterful and atmospheric inns in England.

Leave the Black Bear and follow the main street through Tewkesbury, past rows of higgledy-piggledy half-timbered buildings jettied out over the street. At the far end of the town is the honey-coloured stone of Tewkesbury Abbey. Rebuilt after the battle of Tewkesbury, it was one of the few to escape destruction

The archetypal English pub – Ye Olde Black Bear, Tewkesbury

in the wake of the dissolution of the monasteries; the prudent local council acquired it for four hundred pounds.

From Tewkesbury, the route should now be down to the other great city of this part of England, Gloucester. A look round the cathedral, a drink in a couple of classic Gloucester pubs and then on to the beautiful Forest of Dean, one of the prime sites of iron-working in the pre-industrial age. There is only one problem with this particular itinerary; I could not find a classic pub in Gloucester. There are several venerable old inns, but in each one I entered, the half-timbering sat cheek-by-jowl with red flock wall paper, the smell of frying chips lay heavy on the air and there was all the atmosphere and character of a mock-Tudor Portacabin. If someone out there knows a classic Gloucester pub, please let me in on the secret!

BIRMINGHAM &
THE BLACK COUNTRY

S t Albans is one of our most historic cities, the Roman Verulanium, capital of the province of Britannia. The Roman remains, particularly the theatre, are impressive and the massive cathedral dominates the city. St Alban was a Roman soldier, the first English martyr, killed in 303 AD for sheltering a priest who had converted him to Christianity. Offa of Mercia founded the Benedictine Abbey in 739 to commemorate him; the columns in the transepts survive from the Saxon church. The marble shrine in St Alban's Chapel was painstakingly recreated in the nineteenth century from more than two thousand fragments. The fifteenth-century clock tower in the city centre is one of very few that have survived in Britain. French Row, alongside it, was occupied by the Dauphin's troops in 1216 and the tower still houses a curfew bell from 1335. Two great battles in the Wars of the Roses were also fought within sight of it, in 1455 and 1461.

probably in 209 AD

The electrification of the railway line and the opening of the M25 have turned St Albans into a satellite of London, with all the concomitant house price rises and lemming-like commuter rush. The St Michael's area still has a lot of charm, however, from its fine tenth-century church to the inns that lined this important stop on the coaching route from London towards the north-west. The Rose & Crown seems little altered from that era. Walk down through the park behind the Abbey, past the Fighting Cocks, which is yet another in the never-ending list of claimants to the title of England's oldest inn, and alongside the lake. At the far end of the park, turn left and the Rose & Crown is fifty yards away.

One bar has a magnificent open fireplace with a blazing log fire in winter. There are beams, high-back settles on the stone flags and a warm welcome and friendly conversation at the bar. There is a darts area down a step, or you can sit at a table and leaf through the piles of old magazines, in as pleasant and atmospheric a bar as you could wish.

The other bar has plenty of character, too, with another fireplace and more beams and timbers, and it opens out onto a small garden area. It also has a jukebox, so choose your bar according to your mood. The lunchtime food is good, the beer well-kept and in winter you can warm yourself with a glass of punch or mulled wine as well.

Stage coaches paused at the inns of St Michael's before rattling on towards Birmingham. To a casual glance from one of its plethora of motorways, twentieth-century Birmingham may look like the sort of city you could manage pretty well without, but stiffen your sinews and

The Rose & Crown, St Albans – a coaching inn that retains its character in a very different age

Previous page: The timber framing of the Manor House, West Bromwich

The Rose & Crown
Licensees: John & Paula Milligan
St Michael's Street,
St Albans
☎ St Albans (0727) 51903
11 - 3; 5.30 - 11

Benskins Best Bitter; Ind Coope Burton Ale; Taylor Walker Best Bitter

Lunchtime food. Garden.

give it a chance; behind the concrete canyons are many things to see and a couple of excellent pubs as well!

There has been a settlement at the heart of Birmingham since before the Norman Conquest but it was not until the late eighteenth century that a city began to emerge. Like several other urban centres, it sees itself as the country's second city.

Historically, Brummagem was moulded into greatness by a Victorian political élite with strong temperance views. To this day there are large tracts of the city, such as the Cadbury Estate in Bourneville and the Calthorpe Estate in Edgbaston, that are almost entirely publess. There have always been fewer pubs in Birmingham than in any comparable town, and inevitably this has meant that the few pubs which *were* granted licences grew to be enormous.

For seventy-five years from the turn of the century, a succession of Birmingham pubs held the record as the largest fully licensed public house in the country. The first, and most impressive of these was the Bartons Arms, an epic of Victorian overkill.

Birmingham is a city of the motor car. The Austin Morris influence affected not only the shape of its other industries but also the priorities of its thoroughfares. The cars go straight while the people must weave in and out, left and right, up, down and around. To find the Bartons, try to find the A34 Walsall road north out of the city from Lancaster Circus. After a little over a mile you will spot, on your right, a red-brick and sandstone monstrosity, isolated on a reshaped bombsite, now backed by an incongruous windows-and-scaffolding-type box building.

Opened in 1901, the Bartons is almost a parody of itself. An enormous enamel-tiled, snob-screened, polished mahogany, cast-iron, stained glass, engraved mirrored, open-fired beauty of a place. It is Victorian pomposity epitomised. In 1969 the Birmingham City planners wanted to knock it down. They retreated after the onslaught of protest and satisfied themselves by demolishing the rest of Aston instead.

The pub is run by Mitchells and Butlers, part of the Bass group, who own over half the pubs in Birmingham. To their credit, they have ploughed a great deal of money into maintaining the high standards of craftsmanship that are the pub's hallmark. Less worthy has been their tendency, with each act of 'maintainance', to knock holes through the dividing walls. As a result, we now have a single serpentine lounge bar where seven rooms of different character used to be.

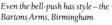

The Victorian splendours of the Bartons Arms, Birmingham

The Bartons Arms
Licensee: Steve Lefevre
High Street,
Aston,
Birmingham
☎ (021) 359 0853
11 - 2.30; 6 - 10.30 (11 Friday & Saturday)

M&B Mild, Brew XI

Lunchtime food (Monday to Friday).

Even the bell-push has style – the Bartons Arms, Birmingham

The use of the rooms upstairs has waned in recent years, though 1930s swing and big band music still features in the 'music hall' on most Fridays. The restaurant is closed at present and food service is confined to pub grub on weekday lunchtimes only.

M&B's two traditional beers are available on handpump. Most real ale enthusiasts have a love-hate relationship with Brew XI, a sweetish, odd-flavoured, light-coloured, unbitter bitter. The deep reddish brown mild ale is a good example of the meaty dark brews that are typical of the industrial West Midlands

To reach our second classic Victorian pub in Birmingham you need to travel about 45° anticlockwise or, to put it another way, two arterial roads to the west. The A457 leaves the Birmingham inner circuit at Paradise Circus and on its way out of town towards the Black Country masquerades as Summer Row, The Parade, Sand Pits, Summer Hill Road, Spring Hill and eventually Dudley Road – a name most Brummies will recognize because it houses one of the city's biggest hospitals. The seventh street on your right after Dudley Road Hospital is Winson Street. Here lies the Bellefield.

If the Bartons is a symbol of Birmingham's glorious past then the Bellefield perhaps more aptly depicts its shaky present. Ten years ago the Bellefield sat half-way along a street of turn-of-the-century terraced houses, the Midlands' answer to Coronation Street's Rovers Return. Five years ago it sat alone, a single surviving, dirty old building in an area that looked like Dresden after the firestorm. Nowadays it plays the part of the olde publicke house in the midst of a brave new housing development that has not yet had time to decay.

The pub reflects its community. It is a multi-racial basic boozer, with a lively public bar and a back room stuck in a time warp: it is as unspoilt a remnant of Victorian interior design as the Bartons, but its upkeep has been less enthusiastic. Like Birmingham itself, it is showy and seedy at the same time.

In the brightly coloured, ornately plastered public, dominated by a carved bar, an impressive ceiling and a noisy television, you will find the sons and daughters of Jamaica and Jullundurpur, of Athlone and the Lozells Road, and quite a few people who come from nowhere in particular.

In the back room, floor to ceiling in green enamel tiling, are framed line drawings of rural pursuits, set in individually designed recesses that have been there as long as the pub itself. There, too, are Winn and Joe, who have used

The Bellefield
Licensee: Sohan Singh
36-38 Winson Street,
Winson Green
Birmingham B18 4JS
☎ (021) 558 0647
11 - 2.30; 5.30 - 10.30 (11 Friday & Saturday)

Davenports Mild, Bitter

Evening barbecues in summer. Garden.

The Bellefield, Birmingham – down-at-heel, but lovable

The fine ceiling in the Bellefield, Birmingham

the Bellefield since the days when it was the White family's home-brew house. Some regulars may have their favourite seats but few, surely, can boast a brass plate erected above their seats for them as a sort of permanent reservation.

The place needs a thorough clean-up. It is not Mr Singh's fault; there is a century of grime ingrained in the leaded windows and around the mantelpieces. A tiled floor needs to be installed, the 1960s gas fire could be replaced, and the hat stand hasn't been polished in decades. It is a lovable place for all this. The beers from the Davenports Brewery in Bath Row are consistently good and on summer evenings they have even opened up a barbecue outside.

From the Bellefield to our next pub involves a remarkable change in atmosphere, both in the pubs themselves and in their surrounding environments, for you are about to enter the areas around the Black Country, an unique urban culture.

To find the Manor House, it is first necessary to find West Bromwich by turning out along the Dudley Road once more and following the signs. From the West Bromwich ring road follow the road to Walsall. After a mile and a half, Hall Green Road will be to your left at a large roundabout. The Manor House is set back from Hall Green Road in what used to be its gardens but are now its car parks.

Unfortunately, the Manor House shows that there definitely can be a difference between a classic pub and a decent pub. The Manor House is the former, but sadly, it no longer has the atmosphere to aspire to the latter.

The building is a superbly reconstructed and

The Manor House
Licensees: Mr & Mrs Walker
Hall Green Road,
Hall Green,
West Bromwich,
West Midlands
☎ (021) 588 2035
11.30 - 2.30; 6 - 10.30 (11 Friday & Saturday)

Banks's Mild, Bitter; Hanson's Black Country Bitter

Lunchtime & evening food. Families welcome. Garden.

overhauled medieval manor house with a baronial hall of impressive proportions. Some years ago, in order to make the building pay its way, a licence was sought and it was converted into a fully functional pub and restaurant. To begin with, it was run by Allied Breweries. Now Wolverhampton and Dudley Breweries, makers of Banks's and Hanson's beers (no relation), have the privilege.

The shell of the building is superb. The nooks and crannies of both floors lend themselves surprisingly well to the purpose of small and medium-sized bar rooms, but alas the decor is monotonous. Each room is appointed in similar fashion to the next: two gross of mass-produced, hoop-backed, clip-on cushion pub chairs are neatly slotted in under half-a-gross of equally boring tables. No attempts have been made to scour junk shops for more solid furnishings.

Hanging twenty feet below the most impressive vaulted ceiling I have seen in a building of half-timbered construction, is a chandelier in the form of a wrought iron wheel hub. Where the candles should be there is a ring of appalling Taiwanese orange-coloured flickering bulbettes, which completely spoil the whole effect.

The Manor House, West Bromwich which is, sadly, better outside than inside

The flagstone floors are covered in large areas by industrial-strength carpeting, as are the ancient, seasoned floorboards. Glaring white lines have been added in gloss paint to demarcate the edges of the broad, shallow steps.

The standard, modern, estate-pub-style bar fittings with whirring electrical beer dispensers do nothing for the atmosphere. Neither do the hosts of hired hands who serve precisely portioned amounts of chopped meat concoctions from plates frazzled by arc lamps, and baby carrots of the 'once deeply frozen and now savagely overboiled' variety. And yes, they really do serve chips with everything.

1970s American-ballad muzak is a compulsory addition to conversation. Even the monk's retreat bar is invaded by 'Your Lying Eyes', 'Surfing U.S.A.' and 'I Never Promised You a Rose Garden'. Sadly, the fruit machines seem quite in place in this particular pub setting.

I am not sure how much the brewery is to blame, how much has been imposed by statutory bodies designed to protect the general public from itself and how much is contributed by the owners of the building, but something, somewhere, is badly awry in what should be one of Britain's great drinking experiences.

Heading back along the Walsall Road to West Bromwich you will eventually find Dudley signposted to your right. In the Black Country proper, all roads lead eventually to Dudley. You should emerge at the Burnt Tree roundabout where the roads from Dudley, Wolverhampton, Birmingham, Oldbury and West Bromwich meet. On your way into the town the next traffic lights mark the top of Tipton Road and it is here that you turn right, in the shadow of Dudley Castle, which houses the famous zoo.

The Bottle and Glass is no longer strictly a pub. It is open only to visitors to the Black Country Museum, in the grounds of which it now stands. The Bottle & Glass started life five miles away in Buckpool, near the Wordsley Hospital. It was built in 1776 as a simple alehouse. By 1977 it had changed hands on a number of occasions and its owners Ansells, part of the Allied Breweries group, deemed it unviable and closed it down. At around the same time the Black Country Museum was being conceived and, a year later, it was agreed that the pub should be taken down brick by brick and reconstructed in its original condition on its present site.

The museum is on the lines of a 'theme park' depicting a Black Country village in the last century. For all its heavy industrial history and closeness to big city Birmingham, this unique part of the West Midlands has always been a collection of village communities. The museum has a cobbled street with typical shops and houses from the nineteenth-century. It has a canal wharf and can offer barge trips down part of the longest canal tunnel in the world. It has a coal mine, a tramway, an old-style funfair and a wide variety of other authentically reconstructed attractions, including craftsmen's workshops that still operate.

The pub keeps to its traditions too. There is no lager and no new-fangled soft drinks, but ginger beer and orange squash, a selection of British spirits, and handpumped mild and bitter beers from the nearby Holden's brewery at Woodsetton are available.

The family room at the back would have been an assembly room in days gone by. The bar and the snug, surely the smallest room in England to boast an inglenook fireplace, are superbly atmospheric. So is the landlord, Bert Tudor, who breathes enthusiasm for his work and for the project as a whole.

The pub re-opened in 1981 having taken nine months to dismantle and a further eighteen months to reconstruct. It is a measure of the perfectionist streak in the Trust members who did the work that they even rebuilt the cellar, which had been in particularly poor condition, to the exact same design and using similar brick, despite the fact that nobody ever sees it except the landlord! In fact the arched design, coupled

The Bottle & Glass
Licensee: Bert Tudor
The Black Country Museum,
Tipton Road,
Dudley,
West Midlands
☎ (021) 557 9643
11 - 2.30 (Mon-Sat); 12-2 (Sun). Bank Holidays till 4.30pm. 6.30 - 10.30 May to July, Wednesdays only.

Holden's Black Country Mild, Bitter

Lunchtime snacks. Families welcome. Garden. Private parties by arrangement.

The Bottle & Glass, Dudley is a proper pub, not just a museum piece!

with its canalside location makes for excellent natural temperature control for his splendid ales. Food is limited to rolls with cheese and raw onion, the staple diet of previous generations of pub-goers.

I can thoroughly recommend the whole museum, which offers an excellent value day out for all the family.

With exquisite timing I arrived at our next classic town pub within days of a change of landlord, local opinion informing me that the move had occurred under an unspecified cloud. Officially named the Vine, it is known to all as the Bull & Bladder. It is an archetypal Black Country boozer, the brewery tap for the Daniel Batham brewery in Brierley Hill.

To reach the Bull & Bladder, go through Dudley town centre and out along the Stourbridge road until you spot the turning to Brierley Hill High Street. At the end of the High Street there is a sharp left turn, almost back on itself, into Delph Road. Batham's Delph Brewery is unmistakable, sharing the same frontage as the Bull & Bladder.

The Batham family own only eight pubs and the family business is a close-knit concern, some of their licensees being in their third decade of tenancy. In its time the Bull & Bladder has been through highs and lows and I have decided to include it here in the hope that a new tenant will see it right once more.

The brightly painted frontage used to boast 'Blessings of your heart. You brew good ale'

The Vine (The Bull & Bladder)
Licensee: Mr S.M. Suttie
Delph Road,
Brierley Hill,
West Midlands
11 - 2.30; 6 - 10.30 (11 Friday & Saturday)

Bathams Mild, Bitter; Delph Strong Ale (winter)

Lunchtime & evening snacks. Families welcome. Garden.

The Bull & Bladder – Batham's characterful brewery tap

(Shakespeare). The windows proclaim the long association with the Royal and Ancient Order of Buffaloes. Inside at the time of my visit, the four bars looked bare. The long bar, where the jazz bands played, seemed sad and lifeless, and the family room was as shabby and unused as ever I remember it, but the beer was still bright and sweet and flavoursome, fat rolls filled the plate and the pub clearly had not died yet. It will be a great challenge for whoever takes it on.

Most people come for the beer and the indefinable 'atmosphere', but the latter has, in a way, been the pub's own worst enemy. Just because a place is vibrant with chatter does not mean you let it go without improvements. A backyard, two legal family rooms, four bars, a reputation for good live music and first rate ales should surely add up to more than this.

It was in the Bull & Bladder some years ago that I witnessed a priceless moment. While waiting to be served at the hatch I heard the unmistakable wailing of an unweaned infant pierce the air in the sparsely inhabited Family Room. As I turned its mother leant over its carry cot and in a strong Black Country accent intoned: 'Yow wotch yow mouth or oy wown't bring yow ere again.'!

From the Delph Brewery cross over the first junction and take a left at the end of the road, turning right immediately thereafter. With luck this will bring you to Coppice Lane which becomes Saltwells Road. When this meets the Halesowen to Dudley road turn left towards Netherton. On reaching the first

The Old Swan, Netherton is universally known as 'Ma Pardoe's'

serious block of shops you will see the legendary Old Swan (known locally as 'Ma Pardoes') to your right. There is a car park behind the pub in Northfield Road.

The Pardoe family connection with the pub only began in 1935 when it was purchased by the late Fred Pardoe. His widow Doris took over its management when Fred died in the early 1950s and remained licensee until her death in 1984, though in latter years she had played little part in its day-to-day running. 'Pardoe's' home-brew, the distinctive light, flowery beer that made the place internationally renowned, has always been brewed by George Cooksey, who brews there still.

On the death of Mrs Pardoe it became clear that the traditional way of running the business had relied, as is often the case in family businesses, on a great deal of good will and minimal overheads. At one stage the business looked certain to be purchased by a big national brewer intent on cashing in on the name whilst at the same time wrecking the pub. But then a consortium, which included CAMRA, bought the pub and set about keeping the business viable whilst limiting the damage to our heritage. It is now owned and run by the independent Hoskins brewery.

Since the 'takeover', the company has expanded the Old Swan by adding three new bar areas. These have been created by purchasing the house next door and knocking the two properties into one. It also gives the pub five coal fires, which must be a record!

Upstairs, the dingy old function room has been converted to take private parties. The old menu of ham or cheese rolls has been expanded to include faggots and peas and other traditional pub foods. Plans are afoot to create a legal family room inside the pub that will not interfere with customers in the other bars, and there is now room to sit outside at the back. The brewery continues as it always has done and can be viewed at reasonable times, though a 'phone call in advance is advisable.

From one fine home-brew pub, make the short journey to one of the cradles of the Industrial Revolution, where, nearby, you can sample the home-brewed ales of another classic pub. Abraham Darby brought a fortune to himself and fame to Coalbrookdale, an obscure area of Shropshire, by setting up the first iron-smelting works to use coke instead of charcoal, early in the eighteenth century. The nearby Ironbridge takes its name from the bridge spanning the Severn, the first in the world to be constructed from iron. The previously sylvan setting of Coalbrookdale and its

The Old Swan
Licensee: Val Chapman
Halesowen Road,
Netherton,
West Midlands
☎ Dudley (0384) 53075
11 - 2.30; 6 - 10.30
(11 Friday & Saturday)

Mrs Pardoe's Home Brew;
Guest beers

Lunchtime & evening food
(Monday to Saturday,
12 - 2; 6.30 - 9). Families
welcome. Outside drinking
area.

Function room. Music
upstairs weekends and
Tuesdays, Jazz Thursdays

environs was swiftly transformed by the smelt mills of the iron masters. Anna Seward, writing in 1785, described a

'Scene of superfluous grace, and wasted bloom
O, violated Colebrook!
. . . hear, in mingled tones,
shout their throng'd barge, their pond'rous engines clang
Through thy coy dales; while red the countless fires,
With umber'd flames, bicker on all thy hills,
Dark'ning the Summer's sun with columns large
Of thick, sulphureous smoke, which spread like palls,
That screen the dead, upon thy sylvan robe
Of thy aspiring rocks; pollute thy gales,
And stain thy glassy waters.'

The industry that created this vision has long moved on. Ironbridge and its surroundings are greener now, though the industrial past is preserved and evoked in the industrial museums in and around the town.

The first iron bridge in the world, at the heart of 'violated Colebrook'

Our next classic pub is a typical nineteenth-century mineworkers' and foundrymens' slaker, which also makes its own modest contribution to the area's history; it is one of only four home-brew pubs surviving from before their re-emergence into fashion in the 1970s and 1980s.

Drive to Madeley, just to the south of Telford, then take the old Coalport Road from Madeley Church and you will not miss the fading Union Jack signs of the All Nations. If you get on the new Coalport Road by mistake, turn off where you see a sign to a pub called the Pheasant – it is right next door to the All Nations.

The old bridge alongside the pub once carried an early, inclined coal railway across the valley. A continuous rope connected the pit at the top of the hill with the other side of the valley. Coal wagons at the top of the incline were filled with coal and, as they descended, the weight of the laden wagons pulled the empty ones back up to the top.

The All Nations is absolutely unspoilt, its single room unaltered for many years. There are no frills, no muzak, no food and no electronics, just some delicious beer and good conversation. Outside is a terrace and a rose garden. Old barrels serve as tables and you can enjoy both the home-brewed ale and the twentieth-century peace of an area now green once again after its black industrial past. Our next journey takes us to an area where the scars of the Industrial Revolution were later and even deeper.

The All Nations
Licensee: Mrs E. Lewis
Coalport Road,
Madeley,
Shropshire
☎ Telford (0952) 585747
12 - 2.30; 7 - 11

All Nations Pale Ale

'KING COTTON' &
THE NORTH WEST

If Ironbridge was the cradle of the Industrial Revolution, Manchester and the North-West was the place where its effects, both good and ill, were perhaps most dramatically felt. 'King Cotton' brought phenomenal expansion and enormous wealth to the cotton towns and cities, but the wealth did not spread far down the social classes and the population of the teeming slums often lived in the most appalling conditions.

The change from charcoal to coal for smelting had already shifted the focus of iron production from its traditional areas in the Weald of Sussex and the Forest of Dean to the West Midlands; the development of the steam engine and improvements in transport through canals, and later railways, shifted the focus of other industries to areas with good access to coal and to viable transport routes. Before turnpiking, much transport was carried out by pack horses, often doubling the cost of heavy goods such as coal in a few miles. Even turnpikes, which made the transport of goods by horse-drawn wagon more possible, had only a marginal effect on transport costs compared to the coming of the canals and railways.

The first great canal in Britain was built for the Duke of Bridgewater, connecting his mines at Worsley with the hungry mills of Manchester. It was later extended to link with Liverpool as well. Its tomato soup-coloured waters are still much-used by pleasure boats today, though it has virtually no commercial use. The late eighteenth century saw a wave of canal building, but scarcely had the Canal Age dawned than it was swept away by the coming of the railways. The Liverpool-Manchester railway line opened in 1830, just five years after the pioneering Darlington-Stockton line, and signalled the beginning of the end both for the canal and coaching ages.

The coaching age is commemorated in the name of one Manchester pub, however, and that will be our first call, at the uniquely named Peveril of the Peak.

It was built in 1825 by James Grundy, a driver one of the four main Manchester to London stagecoaches, called the Peveril of the Peak. Passengers paid a fare of a shilling for each coachman and half-a-crown to five shillings to the guard. Most of the stagecoach drivers were, no doubt, honest men, passing on the receipts to the company; Mr Grundy was not and did not. His illicit profits were sufficiently large for him to buy land and build the pub, which he named, probably with his tongue in his cheek, after the stagecoach that made his enterprise possible.

The 'Pev' has a beautiful, green-tiled exterior,

The Peveril of the Peak
Licensee: Teresa Swanick
127 Great Bridgwater Street, Manchester
11.30 - 3; 5.30 - 11

Webster Yorkshire Bitter, Choice; Wilsons Original Bitter

Food: pies & sandwiches only. Outside drinking area.

Previous page: The stained glass in Liverpool's alternative 'cathedral' – the Vines Hotel!

The nineteenth-century Peveril of the Peak, Manchester – surrounded by twentieth-century developments

with a fine, art-nouveau, tiled frieze. Inside is a central bar with much stained glass and wood. The public bar has a curved, carved wood bar, and a great rarity, a table football machine. Off the main bar is a room with pool table, dartboard and juke box, and a small plush room with a fine Victorian fireplace with inset tiles.

The next classic pub lies on the other side of the city centre, and is a suitably grand monument to the wealth and civic pride of Victorian Manchester. The city's expansion in the nineteenth century was almost incredible. At the time of the first official census in 1801 the population of Manchester and Salford was 84,000; in 1851 it had risen to 367,000. Such phenomenal expansion led to great pressure for housing; it was met by speculative builders constructing thousands of back-to-backs, defective in materials, quality of workmanship, basic amenities and sanitation. For the first time, the industrialists no longer lived by their factories; the mills were sited in working-class districts, while the middle-classes lived elsewhere. This change was noted by Benjamin Disraeli who wrote of 'Two nations; between whom there is no intercourse and no sympathy; who are as ignorant of each other's habits, thoughts and feelings as if they were dwellers in different zones, or inhabitants of different planets.' Engels in his 'Condition of the Working Class in England', written in the same year, 1845, noted: 'He who visits Manchester simply on business or for pleasure need never see the slums, mainly because the working-class districts and the middle-class districts are quite distinct.' Engels went on to describe the Manchester slums, talking of 'a degree of dirt and revolting filth the like of which is not to be found elsewhere. The worst courts are those leading down to the Irk, which contain unquestionably the most dreadful dwellings I have ever seen.'

In order that you can enjoy the next classic pub to the full, I will spare you further details from Engels' account, but it is a timely reminder, perhaps, of the reasons why so many sought alcoholic oblivion in the 'gin palaces' of the Victorian industrial towns and cities.

The Crown & Kettle is a fine example of the genre, almost next to the Express building and a journalists' local for many years. Recently restored to its full gothick splendour, it was originally the stipendiary court and was first granted a licence in 1799. Some of the more excitable locals claim that hangings were actually carried out where the entrance to the pub now stands. It is also claimed that the pub is haunted by the ghost of one of the judges from the court, who used to live on the upper floors.

The Crown & Kettle
Licensee: Brian Mair
2 Oldham Road,
Ancoats,
Manchester
☎ (061) 236 0227
11.30 - 3; 5.30 - 11

Webster Yorkshire Bitter, Choice; Wilsons Original Bitter

Lunchtime food. Families welcome.

The Crown part of the name comes from its courtroom days; no-one knows where the Kettle comes from. There is an L-shaped bar area with a food servery in one part and a pool table sited in the other. The ceiling is one of the most remarkable you will ever encounter. It is unusually high for a pub and almost incredibly elaborate, with bizarre, fluted protuberances that presumably once held chandeliers. Off the bar is a small snug with a fireplace and another curiosity – the panelling on the walls was originally in the R100 airship.

Across the road is one of Victorian England's most venerable institutions, a Yates Wine Lodge. The original was lost in a fire and replaced by a new and squeaky-clean version. Virtually all the Lodges have now been spruced up by Yates' thrusting young management; no doubt the commercial results justify the change, but true aficionados preferred to drink their Yates draught Australian wines in the traditional scrubbed wood surroundings, amongst a company that always came as cosmopolitan and bohemian as you could wish. The Yates story is a remarkable one, but the full version must await another book, another day.

Manchester city centre, like most of industrial Britain, was given a thorough going-over by 1960s developers, but they missed many of the remarkable Victorian warehouses just off Piccadilly, in the heart of the city. Again, like many other cities, many of the most interesting architectural features are high above street level and often pass unnoticed. The Town Hall is a remarkable piece of Gothic revival architecture by Alfred Waterhouse, containing fine paintings by Ford Madox Brown. The public library looks more like school of Albert Speer, but Manchester has several superb libraries and museums, which will happily fill those long hours waiting for the pubs to open.

When you have seen enough of Manchester, head out to the east, through Ashton under Lyne to Stalybridge, a town with a most unusual classic pub.

The Buffet Bar, Stalybridge Station – a genuine pub with a genuine pub dog

Follow the signs to the station in Stalybridge, for that is where you will find the next classic pub, on the east-bound platform. It is, in fact, the station buffet. It is a bit of pre-Thatcherite privatisation that few would argue with, for the result has been to produce a station buffet that also has all the character and atmosphere of a proper pub, though its regulars do keep disappearing abruptly into the night as their trains pull in!

There is a long marble-topped counter, a fireplace with a coal stove, and a paperback library. The walls are decorated with railway

memorabilia. If you are not in the mood for the excellent range of beers, then tea, coffee, Bovril, Horlicks, hot chocolate and soup are also available. The station has a surprisingly large flow of passengers. It is a junction of the Manchester-Leeds line with a branch line to Stockport and, during licensing hours, many travellers find time to call in at the station buffet to share a drink with those who are not travelling anywhere, just enjoying a classic pub.

Beerophiles will find the whole of the Manchester area a delight for both their taste-buds and their wallets. It is the home of a number of vigourously independent brewing companies, all producing delicious beer at very reasonable prices. Boddingtons, Burtonwood, Holts, Hydes, Lees, Moorhouse's, Oldham and Thwaites all have their devotees, but many argue that Robinsons is the best of the lot. To find out if they are right, you will need to travel to Stockport, to the next classic pub. Starting from the Stalybridge Station Buffet, the train is really the only way to go, but if you must drive, go back into Ashton and then follow the Stockport signs.

The Stockport parish church makes a useful landmark for locating the Bakers Vaults. If you are driving, park just above the church and walk down, through or round the market hall, to the pub. There are street markets on Fridays and Saturdays and a flea market on Tuesdays, and the pub can be as lively as the market outside.

A long, high, central bar, with old wooden

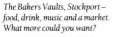

The Bakers Vaults, Stockport – food, drink, music and a market. What more could you want?

The Buffet Bar
Licensee: Ken Redfern
Platform 1,
Stalybridge Station
Stalybridge,
Greater Manchester
☎ (061) 338 2020

Linfit Enoch's Hammer; Moorhouse's Bitter; Taylor Landlord, Ram Tam

Lunchtime & evening snacks. Families welcome. Outside drinking area (the station platform!).

spirit barrels above it, divides the pub. There are high arched windows and wooden partitions dividing the seating into more intimate areas. The resident chef at the Bakers Vaults provides a fine range of home-made food, all at remarkably reasonable prices. The tables are laid out with fresh flowers, yet the pub is never in any danger of becoming a restaurant, it retains a vibrant pub atmosphere. There is regular, live, blues music a few nights a week, with the piano being pounded on Saturday and Sunday lunchtimes.

The market area is a fast-improving part of Stockport, and the Bakers Vaults is a great place to enjoy the bustle of the market through the day, or good food, good company and good music at night.

If this talk of food has made you ready for lunch, take the A5145 towards Didsbury from Stockport. Where it crosses Kingsway it becomes Wilmslow Road; carry on in towards Manchester until you reach the Royal Oak. There is a large central bar, serving three separate areas; the lounge has its own bar with waitress service in the evenings, but at lunchtimes service is from the main bar.

The rooms are filled with comfortable old wooden chairs and tables with brass rails, and the walls are covered with a fine collection of old theatre and day bills, some dating back over 200 years. Mr Gosling also has excellent collections of antique pottery spirit barrels, coronation mugs, steins, tankards and toby jugs. In the early evenings a selection of appetizers are provided, free of charge, but it is at lunchtime that you will see the Royal Oak in its full glory, for it provides what is quite simply the best, and best value, pub lunch you will find.

There is nothing elaborate about it, just bread and cheese or paté, but the selection of cheeses and patés makes Harrods food hall look understocked, the portions make even the most seasoned trencherman blink and the price is ridiculously low. Add to this, bread that is as moist and tasty as you will find anywhere and Marstons beer that is always in perfect condition and you will understand why it is such a popular pub, day and night. Though there may be hordes in, service is always quick and the quality of the beer and the lunch will make you think seriously about moving to Didsbury.

Enjoy your lunch, then head west through Manchester suburbia, towards Liverpool and two quite remarkable Victorian pubs.

In the 1720s, Defoe was already describing Liverpool as 'now become so great, so populous and so rich, that it may be called the Bristol of this part of England . . . and in a

The Royal Oak, Didsbury – good beer and the best pub lunch you will ever eat

The Bakers Vaults
Licensees: Ian & Dot Brookes
Market Place,
Stockport
☎ (061) 480 3182
11.30 - 3; 5.30 - 11

Robinsons Mild, Best Bitter

Lunchtime & evening food. Families welcome. Regular live music.

The Royal Oak
Licensee: Arthur Gosling
729 Wilmslow Road,
Didsbury,
Manchester
☎ (061) 445 3152
11 - 3; 5.30 - 11

Marston Mercian Mild, Bitter, Pedigree

Lunchtime food. Outside drinking area.

little time may probably exceed it, both in commerce and in numbers of people', and the nineteenth-century expansion of Liverpool was even more dramatic than that of Manchester. The population grew from 78,000 to 376,000 in the first fifty years of the century, actually overtaking Manchester as Lancashire's most populous city. Defoe talked of a harbour that could hold a thousand sailing ships at once, and it was as a great port that Liverpool grew rich on the growing North American trade, first in slaves and later in the cotton that disappeared into the voracious Lancashire mills.

Liverpool has had more than its fair share of industrial and social troubles in recent years, but its reputation is worst among those who do not know the city; its wealth of fine buildings are part of its appeal, but there is also a cosmopolitan air and a warmth and wit among its natives that gives Liverpool a vitality that some of our more boring cities will never be able to match. All that, the Beatles and our two most successful football teams too!

The city has two cathedrals, either one of which would be impressive enough for most cities. The neo-Gothic Anglican cathedral is the largest Anglican church in Britain with a 9,700-pipe organ, which is the largest in the world. In the graveyard is the grave of the first person in the world to die in a railway accident. The Roman Catholic cathedral, begun in 1933 with Lutyens' firm intention of building the largest church in Europe, and restarted in 1962 to a less gigantic and more contemporary plan, is one of the few examples of modern architecture that is almost universally admired.

The city also has several notable Victorian temples to Mammon, including the Royal Liver, Cunard and Mersey Docks Board buildings, and the St George's Hall is another must. For those interested in pubs, there are two superb topers' cathedrals as well.

Victorian soft porn at the Vines Hotel, Liverpool

The Vines is an unmistakable Liverpool landmark. Turn left out of Lime Street Station or walk down from the St John's Precinct car park and you will see its massive tower and its clock jutting out over the street. The clock is one of only two in the country by its designer; the other is Big Ben. The Vines' frontage with its marble facia with huge curved, etched and brilliant cut windows, gives you an idea of the splendours inside.

There is a magnificent room with lovely woodwork and a remarkable ceiling of bas relief satyrs' heads gazing down on the drinkers below, though the more recent bar is an intrusive feature. Off the corridor is a smoke room with bench seats divided by wood partitions and

The Vines Hotel
Licensee: Frank Randles
81 Lime Street, Liverpool
☎ (051) 709 3977
11.30 - 3.30; 5 - 10.30 (11 Friday & Saturday)

Walker Dark Mild, Bitter, Best Bitter

Lunchtime food. Families welcome at lunchtime.

another ornate ceiling, and at the other side of the main bar is a magnificent, bow-fronted bar, clad in brightly polished copper. There is a vast fireplace of marble and copper, flanked by carved wooden figures, and beyond it a room with another marvellous fireplace, seating divided into booths by wood and stained glass partitions, and reliefs of cherubs around the top of the walls. Over the fire is a plaster relief of Norse longships.

Across the corridor is another remarkable room, with an unique and very beautiful stained-glass skylight. The panelled walls are hung with oil paintings on loan from the City's Walker Art Gallery, and there is yet another vast fireplace. The room can be hired for a variety of functions and is also used as a servery for lunchtime food, though it seems a little prosaic to be nibbling on a toasted sandwich in these grandiose surroundings!

The Vines is one of several fine Victorian and Edwardian pubs in the city that have been carefully restored by Walkers, the Liverpool arm of Allied Breweries; the other Liverpool classic is an equally remarkable pub, a tribute to the brother company, Tetleys. As Lady Bracknell perhaps ought to have said, for Liverpool to have one such pub is acceptable, but two smacks of greed! The only jarring note in both is the presence of a large number of ugly, modern, electronic machines.

The Philharmonic is on the corner of Hope and Hardman Street, just across from the Philharmonic Hall. After the Vines, the Philhar-

Even the Gents is a work of art in the Philharmonic Hotel, Liverpool

monic's carved stone and etched and cut glass may seem almost unassuming. Enter through the fine, wrought-iron entrance gate beneath the motto 'Pacem Amo'.

Inside is an island bar, with a magnificent mosaic front. There is a mosaic floor, superb stained glass, intricately carved mahogany, copper reliefs and a fine fireplace. The Brahms and Liszt rooms (terribly subtle these Merseysiders!) have fireplaces and wood panelling. Beyond them is the Grandé lounge, with another fireplace, plaster reliefs of classical undraped women above the wood panelling and two rather grimy, stained glass skylights. The room acts as the food servery at lunchtime. In the evenings it often features live music – jazz and rock, each two nights a week.

There are a succession of snugs and small rooms off the main bar area, and the public bar, with a couple of fine old cash registers and a glass screen making a small private area at one end. There is a tiny snug just beyond it. The other great sight in the Philharmonic is the Gents toilet, truly a cathedral among Gents, though the ceiling looked in need of some repair work on my visit. Liverpool also has a Yates Wine Lodge nick-named with typical Liverpudlian wit 'The In Off'. It stands next to a police station and, if you are not used to the Australian wine, you may go in off the white!

To complete a quartet of remarkable Merseyside pubs, leave Liverpool to the north, past the Aintree racecourse, home of the Grand National, and make for Lydiate.

Turn off the A59 onto the A567 through Lydiate. The Scotch Piper is on the left-hand side, immediately after the petrol station. It is a beautifully thatched pub with summertime flower baskets hanging on its white-washed walls and inside you will find all the character and atmosphere you would expect from the 'oldest pub in Lancashire', dating from 1320 AD. It has been so sensitively and carefully restored that it recently won a major award from CAMRA's Pub Preservation Group.

Sit outside at the tables on the forecourt or on the grass at the rear of the pub, or sample the superb atmosphere inside. The small bar has beams, fine old oak benches and an open fire. Its tiny servery opens onto the ground floor cellar, where the beer is stillaged, ready to be served straight from the cask. There is another room with beams, oak pillars, bench seats, including 'cubby-hole' seats either side of the fireplace and a dartboard. At the end of the pub is the best room, with carpets and cushioned seats, but the place to be is the bar, enjoying the atmosphere and the 'crack'.

The Philharmonic Hotel
Licensees: Edward & Julie Smithwick
36 Hope Street,
Liverpool
☎ (051) 709 1163

Tetley Mild, Bitter

Lunchtime food. Families welcome.

The Scotch Piper
Licensees: Charles & Ada Rigby
Southport Road,
Lydiate,
Merseyside
11.30 - 3; 5.30 - 10.30 (11 Friday & Saturday)

Burtonwood Mild, Bitter

Food: sandwiches only. Garden.

The superbly restored Scotch Piper, Lydiate

The pub allegedly got its name from one of the followers of Bonnie Prince Charlie, who was wounded and brought to the inn, then called the Royal Oak, to recover. He fell in love with and married the daughter of the house, and in his honour the name was changed to the Scotch Piper.

Just up the road is another very different, but equally classic pub. Drop back onto the A59 and drive north to Ormskirk, to the Buck i'th' Vine.

You will find the pub very close to the parish church. Burscough Street is pedestrianised, however, so park in the public car park and walk through the archway to the pub. There are tables where you can sit and drink in the yard, surrounded by the old stables and the building which once housed the pub brewery. At the front is a cobbled area where you can sit to admire the old brick frontage of the pub. The oldest part dates back to around 1650 and the main corridor through the pub used to be an alleyway with a window into the tiny bar from which beer was served. Though it is now closed in, it preserves much of the atmosphere of that era.

There is a delightful snug behind the bar with leather seats, Britannia tables and a fine wooden fireplace with copper and tiles. The smoke room has a fireplace, beams, shelves of old books and old brewery signs.

There is another room off the corridor also with a fireplace, and at the back is a room with shelves and high stools where you can play darts, sit and chat, or even play the piano. The room is also used for other sorts of music – a folk club on Thursday nights and occasional live music at other times.

This serving hatch was once a window, opening onto the street – the Buck i'th' Vine, Ormskirk

The Buck i'th' Vine
Licensees: Chris & Carol Potter
Burscough Street,
Ormskirk,
Lancashire
☎ Ormskirk (0695) 72647
11.30 - 3 (4 Thursdays);
5.30 - 11

Walker Dark Mild, Bitter, Best Bitter

Lunchtime food 12 - 2, Tuesday-Saturday. Families welcome. Outside drinking areas.

BURTON ALE, SHEFFIELD STEEL & BRADFORD WOOL

We have already travelled to the west of the Pennines where 'King Cotton' ruled Lancashire. Our next journey leads us to South and West Yorkshire, homeland of the steel and wool textile industries, calling along the way at the great cities of the East Midlands – Leicester, Nottingham and Derby – and, most importantly in a book about pubs, the capital of British brewing, Burton.

The route linking all these places is the M1, which signalled the dawn of the motorway age in Britain. Follow it north, as fast as the law, the traffic and the seemingly never-ending road works will allow. Beyond the M6 turn-off, life on the M1 becomes a bit more tolerable. Reward yourself for your endurance in getting this far by turning off at junction 21, to Leicester and its classic pub. Leicester is one of the oldest towns in Britain, its Celtic origins far pre-dating the Roman township. The Guildhall, the Jewry Wall and the Norman Hall of the castle are well worth seeing, while devotees of English history may wish to travel to Market Bosworth a few miles west of the city, where Henry Tudor gained his decisive victory over Richard III.

To reach the classic Leicester pub, follow the Loughborough ring road signs until you reach Abbey Lane. If you are travelling from the city centre, take the A6 towards Loughborough and Derby. In either event, go down Abbey Lane, straight across the traffic lights at Abbey Park Road, then turn right at the next lights into Corporation Road and immediately left into Beaumanor Road, where you will find the Tom Hoskins.

The Tom Hoskins is a brand new pub, opened in 1984 as the brewery tap in what was once the Hoskins' family living room. The pub began with a single public bar, which was 'just a shade above spit and sawdust,' according to the licensee. The taproom remains right in that 'back to basics' mould; stone and board floors and stripped wood benches, with decor mainly consisting of beer mats from the two hundred or so breweries from which the Tom Hoskins has had guest beers in the few years since it opened.

After running for a couple of years with just this basic public bar, a new, more comfortable, lounge area, the Grist Room, was added for those who wanted rather more comfort and some carpet on the floor! Wrought-iron gates lead into the stone-flagged area surrounding the bar, while the rest of the room is carpeted, with wood-panelling and comfortable seats. It was created out of the old office, malt store and grist mill and to commemorate its earlier use, an

Previous page: Cock of the North – the Cock & Bottle, Bradford

The Tom Hoskins
Licensee: Anthony Diebel
131 Beaumanor Road,
Leicester.
☎ Leicester (0533) 681160
11.30 - 2.30; 5.30 (6
Saturday) - 11

Hoskins Mild, Bitter, Penns, Premium, Old Nigel (October-March); Guest beers

Lunchtime food. Garden. Hospitality/function room.

effigy of the miller with a sack of barley stands at the head of the hoist, above the Grist Room. The effigy is modelled on Alf Taylor, one of the Tom Hoskins' regulars, usually to be found behind a hand of dominoes in the taproom.

Dominoes and darts are the only regular re-creations available at the pub, apart from the pleasures of friendly conversation and the excellent ale, but it plays a full part in the life of its community, with a bonfire night party, and St Andrew's day celebrations that include haggis, a piper, low-priced whisky and Scottish guest beers. Aficionados of pool tables, juke boxes and fruit machines will have to look elsewhere, however, this is an electronics-free zone!

The Tom Hoskins, Leicester – a classic pub with beer brewed in a 'working museum'

There is a sheltered, walled garden outside where families are welcome if the weather permits and you can also see the well from which the brewery used to draw its water. Inside is a small re-creation of a Victorian street, with a post box and a shop window with many old bottles of beer on show.

The Hoskins beer is brewed on site in a Victorian brewery that operates as a working museum. Visitors are welcome to tour this, one of the country's last surviving traditional cottage breweries. As well as the brewing process, you can see eighteenth- and nineteenth-century cooper's tools, cask branding irons and a 1930s bottling plant that is still in working order.

When you leave the Tom Hoskins, take the A50 west of Leicester, across the M1, towards Burton upon Trent. Almost as soon as you leave the urban sprawl behind, you are into rich farmland, with field after field of barley ripening under whatever sun is available in the British summer. Pass through the pleasant market town of Ashby de la Zouch, with a name that delights all tourists, and yet more acres of barley surround you, signalling the importance of Burton as a brewing centre long before you come in sight of it.

When you reach Burton, cross the Trent, pausing, if you wish, at the excellent Burton Bridge Brewery tap, and then drive in towards the city centre until you pick up a sign to the Bass Brewing Museum. If you have a consuming interest in beer, pause for a look round the Museum, which details the reasons why Burton became pre-eminent in British brewing and why Bass was, arguably, the king of them all at one time. CAMRA members and others with a memory for the way Bass used to taste will shed a silent tear at the sight of the Burton Union system, now a museum exhibit rather than a working part of the Bass brewery, though, to be fair, Draught Bass has shown signs in recent years of returning to its magnificent best. You will find that our next classic pub is the perfect place to put this to the test.

It is just behind the Bass Brewery, which is not hard to find, though beware of following your nose, for Burton has several breweries and the smell of brewing is carried on the breeze whichever way the wind is blowing; what made Milwaukee famous had long before provided a bonanza for Burton.

The Cooper's Tavern was at one time the annexe of the Bass Brewery, used as a bottling room, but it has been a pub since the turn of the century. It sits on a one-way street just behind the brewery and, if you are driving, you may have the frustration of lapping it a couple of times before you find the way in.

The old brick exterior has been spruced up and has flower baskets hanging from it in summer. Inside is a front room with leather-covered bench seats, two fireplaces, a dartboard and a piano. Beyond this is the hub of the place, the small taproom with high wood benches, disused barrels for tables and a row of still-used barrels stillaged behind the bar. From them comes as good a pint of Draught Bass as you will encounter anywhere; it is the only pub in the brewing capital that serves draught beer straight from the cask. The clientele is an excellent mix of city gents, working men and students, and the 'crack' around the bar can be as good and sparkling as the beer.

The wallpaper in the front bar has seen better days – the landlord himself describes the decor as 'tatty' – but the Cooper's Tavern is a classic pub, a warm and welcoming old-fashioned local, where you can drink an excellent pint of beer and discover for yourself why Burton became the brewing capital of Britain. In a pub redolent of pub tradition, there is even a traditional pub dog, and a traditional Staffordshire breed at that, a bull terrier.

On leaving the Cooper's, drive to the top of the street, turn left and as soon as you have passed the station and crossed over the railway, turn right into Derby Street, which will lead you straight to the A38, a fast dual carriageway to Derby.

Follow the main road in towards Derby and once more the spires of the cathedral signal your approach to the City. When you reach the inner ring road, follow it and turn right into Abbey Street at a set of traffic lights. Derby's first classic town pub is on the right, a few hundred yards up the street.

The Olde Spa derives its name from the fact that a local physician, Dr Chauncey, discovered a thermal spa in the area in 1733. According to Simpson's *History of Derby* 'about twenty yards

The Coopers Tavern, in the capital city of British brewing – Burton upon Trent

The Cooper's Tavern
Licensee: Tony Henson
43 Cross Street,
Burton upon Trent,
Staffs.
☎ Burton (0283) 32551
10.30 - 2.30; 5.30 (7 Saturday) - 11

Draught Bass

Lunchtime food. Evening snacks. Families welcome at lunchtimes & until 8pm.

The Olde Spa, Derby has been restored with loving care

below the spa he made a handsome cold bath and some rooms to it'. The spa must have been close to the present pub, because mid-nineteenth-century maps show the spa as almost the only building in an area of green fields. Derby has long since spread out to swallow up the surrounding fields, but the Spa survives as a delightful pub.

It is set back from the road by a few yards and has a lovely little beer garden in the shade of a tree, surrounded by roses and honeysuckle in the season, and safely fenced off from the car park and the road. Also in summer there are flowers in baskets and tubs around the door, and more roses growing along the edge of the car park. The inside of the Spa has been completely restored, but it has been done with great care and attention to detail. Though the pub has been opened out to some extent, it still retains three distinct drinking areas, one with a fine cast-iron fireplace, another with a piano in frequent use and a third where those eating tend to congregate. It is light and airy, and popular with all sorts of customers.

Leaving the Olde Spa, drive up to the top of the street, turn left and follow the inner ring road back into the city centre. Derby was a major trading centre as early as the twelfth century and its importance in Britain's industrial development is indicated by the Old Silk Mill industrial museum, which stands on the site of the earliest factory in England, built in 1718-22. It was five or six storeys high and used water power from the River Derwent. The more

Ye Olde Spa Inne
Licensee: Peter Frame
204 Abbey Street, Derby
☎ Derby (0332) 43474
11 - 2.30; 6 - 11

Ind Coope Bitter, Burton Ale

Lunchtime food. Families welcome. Garden.

The dolphins at Ye Olde Dolphin Inn, Derby – a motif shared with the nearby cathedral

recent industrial history of Derby has been closely linked with British Railways and Rolls Royce, who have an aero-engine factory in the city, fronted by a superb wrought-iron gate by Robert Bakewell. There is more wrought-iron work by Bakewell in the cathedral, which is extremely close to the other classic Derby pub, the Olde Dolphin.

Whether you look round the cathedral before or after you visit the Olde Dolphin will be determined by the relative strengths of your thirst for ecclesiastical knowledge and your thirst for a drink. The Dolphin is just a few yards along the road from the cathedral and the dolphin motif on the cathedral gates is echoed in the name of the pub and the sign hanging from the wall. The half-timbered pub dates from 1530, making it Derby's oldest. A few years ago it was in less than splendid condition, but it has been carefully and sensitively restored and improved, without ever losing the character that is evident in such an old and splendid pub.

The entrance off the street leads into a passageway running through to a small beer garden at the back. To one side of this passageway are four contrasting rooms, to the other is the tearoom, open from ten in the morning to four in the afternoon. The first of the pub rooms is the public bar, with beams, boarded walls, a fireplace and a dartboard. Up a couple of steps is the Offiler's Room, named after the brewery which once owned this, and a couple of hundred other pubs around Derby. Though the brewery has long since closed down, the Offiler's Room acts both as a modest museum for it and as a very pleasant place to enjoy a drink. Both it and the public bar are lively and occasionally noisy; if you want a quieter drink there is a very pleasant lounge with beams, brasses, an inglenook and dark oak panelling, or an absolutely tiny snug, probably the smallest bar in Derbyshire, with painted, panelled walls and a pretty tiled fireplace.

All old pubs claim a ghost and the Dolphin is no exception. Their 'grey lady' has been seen from time to time and strange things happen in the far cellar, once the room where a local doctor stored bodies before carrying out experiments on them. The gas taps in the cellar are turned off without any human interference – obviously the ghost is a CAMRA member!

Our next stop is in Nottingham, a few miles to the east along the A52, where we shall find one of the most remarkable pubs anywhere in England. The city is universally famous for its links with Robin Hood, an association which it commemorates with such unlovely monuments as the dual carriage-

Ye Olde Dolphin Inn
Licensee: Nigel Barker
Queen Street,
Derby
☎ Derby (0332) 49115
10.30 - 2.30; 6 - 11

Draught Bass; M&B Mild

Lunchtime food. Evening food until 8pm (not Sunday). Tearoom. Beer garden. Families welcome in tearoom.

way named Maid Marian Way, which leads towards the Trip to Jerusalem.

There are as many claimants to the title of 'the oldest inn in England' as there are to be descendants of the Tsar of all the Russias, but Ye Olde Trip to Jerusalem in Nottingham is one of the more convincing candidates. It is also an absolutely outstanding pub, full of history, character and atmosphere, an obligatory stopping point for anyone with even the slightest interest in our pub heritage.

The Trip, as it is affectionately known, seems to grow out of the rock on which Nottingham Castle stands and the back part of the pub and its cellars are actually carved out of the rock. There are many similar caverns elsewhere in the city and it is likely that the cellars of the Trip were at one time connected by underground passageways to other underground dwellings. One passageway that is known of for certain was the tunnel and staircase connecting the inn with the castle high above it.

All manner of nefarious activities were connected with these secret passages: Queen Isabella's lover is said, for example, to have visited her by this route. There are also two concealed chambers, reached by way of vertical fissures in the rock, which were used as hiding places when the inn and its neighbourhood had a particularly unsavoury and lawless reputation. Charles Pearce, the self-styled 'King of Rogues' escaped capture by hiding in the Trip and it was notorious as a refuge of 'cut-purses, vagabonds and ill-conditioned persons'.

The Trip to Jerusalem is named for the Crusaders who paused there for rest and refreshment on their way to the Holy Land. It has been an inn since 1189 AD and was the brewhouse for the castle even before that. It continued to brew its own beers right up to the Second World War and still retains some of the old brewing equipment. It also has a motley collection of curiosities, including a chest with one hundred locks, weapons, a penny farthing, a family bible and even a walking stick that once belonged to Harry Lauder, in a small museum off the upstairs bar.

A broadsword hangs on the black-and-white exterior of the Trip, with signs proclaiming the pub's antiquity. You enter through a small yard and immediately find yourself in one of the most characterful bars you are ever likely to see. There is a stone-flagged floor, smoke-blackened beams and timbers, and a seating area carved from the honey-coloured rock. At the end is an ancient-looking 'Ring the Bull' game, here called 'Baiting the Bull'. The object is to throw a ring attached to a cord, over a bull's horn fixed to the wall, and it is by no means as easy as it looks!

Ye Olde Trip to Jerusalem
Licensee: Janet Marshall
Castle Road,
Nottingham
10.30 - 2.30; 5.30 - 10.30

Everards Old Original; Marston Pedigree; Ruddles Best Bitter; Samuel Smith Old Brewery Bitter; Guest beers

Lunchtime sandwiches. Outside drinking area.

Ye Olde Trip to Jerusalem, Nottingham – one of the finest pubs in England since the time of the Crusades

At the other side of the bar is a comfortable lounge with bench seats, oak beams and panelling, and a blazing open fire. However, the jewel of the Trip to Jerusalem is the upstairs bar, which is usually only open in the evenings, though if the pub is not too busy, the licensees or the staff will often be willing to show visitors round. It is reached up a winding stone stair, sealed off by an iron gate, and is, again, completely carved out of the sandstone. There is a curving, wood-panelled bar, antique furniture in the hollowed-out alcoves, a blackened, wooden 'Parliament' clock and another which tells the time in every part of the world. Dominating the room, though, is a natural chimney, a fissure rising sixty feet up through the rock to the fresh air above. It was still in use as a chimney earlier this century, and was only swept every thirty years or so. The last time it was done, seven-and-a-half tons of soot were removed! The chimney itself has been sealed, but a chink of light shows how high it reached.

The Trip has been in the capable hands of the Marshall family for over one hundred years; the present licensee, Mrs Janet Marshall, will tirelessly tell you the history of the pub and point out some of its more interesting features. There are many other claimants to be the oldest inn in England; none have a fraction of the character and atmosphere of this marvellous pub.

In fine weather you can take your drink into the tiny yard or to a cobbled area outside. The Trip is right next to the Brewhouse Yard, with a museum which can tell you more of the history of the area. The Castle on Castle Rock is now the city museum and art gallery. It is worth a visit, but do not expect to see the castle of the Sheriff of Nottingham, King John and Robin Hood fame. Most traces of that have long disappeared (save for its dungeons – try one of the conducted tours). The Norman castle was destroyed during the Civil War; its Italianate replacement was burned down in the early nineteenth century and the present one dates from 1831.

Nottingham has much historic interest apart from the Robin Hood legends. Charles I raised his standard here during the Civil War and Hargreaves and Arkwright established a cotton-spinning mill at the dawn of the Industrial Revolution. The unemployment and social dislocation caused by the introduction of the machinery of the new industrial age led to great unrest, and Nottingham was the scene of violent Luddite riots in 1811. The medieval Goose Fair is still celebrated in early October and there is much to see in the historic Lace Market area, where we shall find Nottingham's other classic pub.

Opposite: A trap-door beneath the pool table leads to the cavernous cellars of the Old Angel Inn, Nottingham

The Lace Market is one of the oldest and most interesting parts of the city, though not much lace is produced there these days, and the whole area has gone rapidly up-market from its near-dereliction of a few years back. Like the Trip, buildings in the Lace Market made good use of the easily worked sandstone on which they stand, and the whole area is honeycombed with cellars and passages burrowing beneath the streets. Go through the Broad Marsh shopping centre and out into the streets of the Lace Market. Walk through until you reach the Midland Group Arts Centre. Just beyond it, you will find the Old Angel in Stoney Street on the right.

It dates back to at least the early seventeenth century and was originally called the Angel. The 'Old' was added in the early eighteenth century, when another Angel was opened in the city. The building was substantially altered in 1878 but has been virtually untouched since then. Both exterior and interior are solidly functional, with only the occasional decorative feature, such as the marble pillars round the windows.

Inside is a long, narrow tap room, once three separate rooms, plainly furnished with wooden tables, stools and bench seats, and a pool table and dartboard. There is a more comfortable lounge and a small dining-room, open at lunch-times. Upstairs, a small room acts as the headquarters of the Nottingham branch of the Royal Antediluvian Order of Buffaloes, doubling as a meeting room for other societies. Across the hall from this is a large room, once a non-conformist chapel, now finding secular use as a club room. It is also the venue for a traditional music club every Friday night. The bar was made out of the old chapel pulpit by the present landlord – the chapel folk must be spinning in their graves!

The Angel looks a typical nineteenth-century, basic Nottingham boozer; if you want evidence of its great age, you must drop down below ground level. Providing the pub is not too busy, the landlord will be happy to show you round the Angel's remarkable cellars, which are on three levels, dropping deeper and deeper beneath the pub.

At the top level is the present spotless beer cellar. CAMRA buffs may wish to travel no further, but leave them to an earnest discussion on the respective merits of hard and soft spiles, and go down the stairs past a fine piece of Saxon walling built as part of the Saxon fortifications of the city. The fact that this wall is several feet below present street level indicates what a large amount of rubbish our forebears used to dump in the street!

The huge middle cellar was used as an air-raid shelter during the war. Down below it is yet

The Old Angel Inn
Licensee: Colin James Norton
Stoney Street,
Lace Market,
Nottingham
☎ Nottingham (0602) 502303
10.30 - 2.30; 5.30 - 10.30

Home Mild, Bitter

Lunchtime food, evening snacks. Families welcome.

another large, multi-roomed cellar. In the middle is a shaft leading up to the pub – it finishes under the pool table in the tap room. The beer barrels were hauled up through this over the centuries, as is evidenced by the grooves worn in the stone. When Colin Norton took over at the Angel, these cellars were literally full of rubbish and several tons had to be removed to restore them to this superb condition. They would make a magnificent cellar bar, but sadly a fire certificate would never be issued because of the single, precipitous access; they must remain a delightful and completely unexpected glimpse of old Nottingham.

Daniel Defoe in his eighteenth-century *Tour Through The Whole Island of Great Britain* noted these remarkable cellars: 'The town of Nottingham is situated upon the steep ascent of a sandy rock; which is consequently remarkable, for that it is so soft that they easily work into it for making vaults and cellars, and yet so firm as to support the roofs of those cellars two or three under one another; the stairs into which, are all cut out of the solid, though crumbling rock; and we must not fail to have it be remembered that the bountiful inhabitants generally keep these cellars well stocked with excellent ALE; nor are they uncommunicative in bestowing it among their friends as some in our company experienced to a degree not fit to be made a matter of history.' Some things never change . . .

As with all the best old pubs, the Old Angel has a resident ghost. It is in the cellar and is a sufficiently unnerving apparition for the landlord's bull terrier, a breed not noted for timidity, to refuse to go down there.

The Cross Keys, Sheffield – a fine resting place in a last resting place!

From Nottingham, once more follow the M1 north. Near Mansfield you pass close to Hardwick Hall to the east; if you have time for a detour it is one of the most beautiful Elizabethan houses in England. You also pass a succession of collieries, to remind you, if reminder is needed, that you are deep into coal country.

Leave the M1 at junction 31, the A57 turning signed for Worksop, then follow the road in towards Sheffield. When you reach Handsworth, the spire of St Mary's church is the landmark that shows you that you have reached the Cross Keys, for it is the only pub in Great Britain that stands in a cemetery, occupying a corner of the church graveyard.

The Cross Keys is an eleventh-century building and may well have been constructed to house the builders of the church, a common occurrence around the country. In its time it has been a monastic hospice, a coaching inn and a road house, and it is claimed to be the oldest

The Cross Keys
Licensee: Frank Francis-Taylor
100 Handsworth Road, Sheffield
11.30 - 3; 5.30 - 10.30 (11 Friday & Saturday)

Stones Best Bitter

occupied building in Sheffield. Having spent several centuries in secular hands, it was returned to the church at one stage, as the gift of the then owners, the Bamber sisters, but it was later re-sold, for the princely sum of £43.

The Cross Keys' connections with the church were not confined to its intermittent ownership; a tunnel connected the two buildings at the time of the Civil War, and part of it still finds use at the pub cellar. There is also a story that Mary Queen of Scots stayed at the Cross Keys while on the run from the wrath of Elizabeth I.

The white-painted exterior does not suggest that the pub is anything special, but that impression is quickly altered when you step inside. The bar and 'best room' are in the original part of the building, beamed and atmospheric, with oak-slatted benches in the bar and leather seats in the 'best room'. Off the bar is a small room with a dartboard and a little stove. There is also a second, more recent bar, decorated with brasses and old lamps, and housing Frank Francis-Taylor's impressive collection of knives, swords and weapons.

Part of Frank Francis-Taylor's huge collection of brassware at the Cross Keys, Sheffield

Sheffield is, of course, the home of the steel industry in Britain, and despite decades of decline from its former pre-eminence, it remains the centre for high-quality steels and for the cutlery trade. Daniel Defoe, writing in the early eighteenth century, described Sheffield as 'very populous and large, the streets narrow, and the houses dark and black, occasioned by the continued smoke of the forges, which are always at work.' Anna Seward described it in 1785 as:
'. . . smoke involv'd; dim where she stands
Circled by lofty mountains, which condense
Her dark and spiral wreaths to drizzling rains,
Frequent and sullied; as the neighbouring hills
Ope their deep veins, and feed her cavern'd flames'.

The smoke and fumes from hundreds of forges and foundries no longer pollute the Sheffield air, and acres of derelict land now testify to the scale of the steel city's decline. Visit Abbeydale Industrial Hamlet to the south of the city for an idea of the earlier industrial history of the area, and a sight of the original iron hammers dating from 1785, then rejoin the M1 for the drive up into the heartlands of the wool textile industry, the West Yorkshire giants, Bradford and Leeds.

The M1 terminates in Leeds, unofficial capital of West Yorkshire, a city built, like its neighbours, on the wool trade. Each town or city in what used to be known as the West Riding specialized in a particular part of the wool trade and developed its own particu-

Opposite: The splendid interior of 'Whitelock's First City Luncheon Bar', Leeds

lar character as a result. Batley and Dewsbury in the 'heavy woollen' district were the towns where 'shoddy' and rags (collected by the once ubiquitous rag-and-bone men, who traded packets of 'dolly blue' for whitening the washing, and stones that were used to whiten the edge of the stone steps of houses for them) were turned back into fibres ready for re-use.

Bradford was the centre of 'top' making, where the greasy wool was scoured, carded and spun into 'tops' ready to be made into cloth. Huddersfield was the centre for production of the finest quality worsteds for the suitings of Saville Row, Halifax was the capital of carpet production and Leeds was the centre of the ready-to-wear clothing industry and grew rich upon it.

In the eighteenth and nineteenth centuries both Bradford and Leeds expanded at a furious pace and both competed hotly for pre-eminence as West Yorkshire's premier town. Bradford's mistake was to underestimate the importance of the coming of the railway. Leeds became the major railway town, with Bradford relegated to an outpost on a branch line to nowhere. Bradford has never forgiven Leeds for this indignity!

Leeds' two classic town pubs cover the beginning and the height of Leeds' industrial might. Whitelocks, in the city centre, was established in 1715 as Leeds began its expansion from a small town to a great city; the Garden Gate in Hunslet is a superb example of the affluence and self-confidence of the high Victorian era, when the British Empire and British industry were at the height of their powers and when almost every public building was a statement of Victorian power and certainty.

Whitelocks is in a long narrow yard that runs off Briggate, one of Leeds' main shopping streets. If you are on the train, turn right out of the station and walk through until you see Briggate on your left; walk up it and on the left hand side you will find an alley, Turks Head Yard, down the side of Radio Rentals, opposite Debenhams and Littlewoods. If you are driving, park in one of the shoppers' car parks and ask directions to Briggate. You will rapidly discover that the reputation of Yorkshire people for friendliness to strangers is well-deserved.

Turn into Turks Head Yard and you will see Whitelocks' splendid sign across the alley (or ginnel, as it is known in Yorkshire). There are seasonal flower baskets hanging from the walls and wooden benches and tables down one side of the yard, where you can sit and drink in fine weather, or rest while waiting for the pub to open. To the left is the quite magnificent 'Whitelocks First City Luncheon Bar', as the engraved glass door proclaims.

Whitelocks
Licensees: Mark & Alison Clarke
Turks Head Yard,
Briggate,
Leeds
☎ Leeds (0532) 453950
11 - 3; 5.30 - 10.30

Younger's Scotch, IPA, No 3

Lunchtime & evening food. Restaurant. Outside drinking area.

Inside is a fine, curved, tile-fronted bar with lovely old mirrors, brass fittings, plush bench seats and copper-topped Brittannia tables. At one end is the luncheon bar itself: leather seats, wood partitioning, a fine cast-iron fireplace, with a roaring fire on winter days, and tables laid with crisp white linen, where generations of Leeds businessmen have clinched their deals over the Yorkshire puddings.

The menu remains resolutely traditional: roast beef with Yorkshire puddings, roast lamb, four-egg omelettes, devilled kidneys and scotch pot (beef cooked in beer). At lunchtimes you can eat in the luncheon bar or order from a food counter in the main bar; in the evenings the bar food is restricted to snacks and the house speciality – two deliciously light Yorkshire puddings awash on a sea of onion gravy. At the top end of the yard is a second bar, this time 'Victorianised'. You can book it for private parties, otherwise it is open to the public. The Victorian treatment has been carefully done, but why settle for skilful re-creation when you can enjoy the real thing?

There is many a good tune played on an old instrument – the source of a landlord's favourite music, the cash register at the Garden Gate, Leeds

To reach the next Leeds' town classic, drive out of the city down the side of the station, aiming for the A61 to Rothwell. You are now entering Hunslet, which for every patriotic Yorkshireman is the site of one of the county's two 'cathedrals' – Joshua Tetley's brewery. (The other is Headingley, where Yorkshire's other patron saint 'Sir' Geoffrey Boycott, has been known to score the occasional century.) Tetley's Bitter is almost a religion among Yorkshiremen, and it must be served with the correct 'collar' or tight, creamy head, which requires several pulls on a handpump and develops biceps and pectorals without any recourse to the Charles Atlas method. The beer dispensed in this way has a creamy softness to the palate that Yorkshiremen find ambrosial and southerners find incomprehensible; to see what all the fuss is about, head for the Garden Gate, where you will enjoy Tetleys at its very best.

Drive out on the A61 until you see a sign to the right to the Hunslet Centre car park, also signed to Belle Isle and Middleton. Turn right and then immediately right again into Whitfield Street. Whitfield Place is off to the left. Alternatively, turn right but then carry on until you reach the shoppers' car park on the right. Park there and walk down the side of the supermarket to reach the Garden Gate.

It is all but invisible from the surrounding roads because of the new development that has sprung up around it, but the pub itself is an absolute beauty from its superb tiled frontage to its magnificent interior. It was built on a classic

The Garden Gate
Licensees: Lawrence & Mary Graham
3 Whitfield Place
Hunslet,
Leeds
☎ Leeds (0532) 700379
11 - 3; 5.30 - 10.30 (11 Friday & Saturday)

Tetley Mild, Bitter

Lunchtime sandwiches (pie & peas in winter).

The epitome of a fine Victorian 'corridor' pub – the Garden Gate, Leeds

Victorian town pub layout; a central corridor with mosaic floor, tiled walls, mahogany partitioning and beautiful, etched and engraved glass, with the taproom, smoke room, vault and snug off it. The rooms all have fine, cast-iron fireplaces, more mahogany, glass and tilework, while the heart of the pub, the vault at the front, has a stunning, bow-fronted, tiled bar counter, topped with a fine old cash register.

The Garden Gate is one of Tetley's Heritage Inns and has been carefully and sensitively restored. The only disappointment is the Gents; those hoping for a Philharmonic-style cathedral to Thomas Crapper's art will be dismayed to find that this part of the pub is very definitely of the twentieth century!

The Garden Gate is a defiantly traditional pub with a similarly traditional pub clientele; it is not exclusively male, but women are definitely in the minority. You are also in the heart of rugby league territory; the pub runs two teams. The Garden Gate combines all that is best about the Northern character – it is warm, earthy, nononsense, and has no pretensions. Here you can admire not only the beauty of the Victorian decor, but the commonsense of the pub architects of the period, who laid out a pub with five distinct drinking spaces (the corridor is as popular as the rooms) where, whatever your interests or your mood, you will find congenial company, a great atmosphere and some of the best-kept beer you are likely to come across. Enjoy it!

Before leaving Leeds there are two other Tetley pubs worthy of note. The Adelphi, just by the Tetley brewery and a very close second to the Garden Gate for the quality of its decor, and the Albion, out on the Armley Road near the grim Armley Gaol and another fine Heritage Inn. In Leeds centre, you might also like to try the warm and welcoming atmosphere of the Duck & Drake in Kirkgate, one of the Fighting Cocks chain, which we shall meet again in Bradford.

From Leeds, a few miles journey to the west will take you to Bradford. Once the thriving capital of the wool textile industry, with its mill owners and merchants competing to build the most grand monuments to their commercial empires, Bradford has suffered decades of continuous decline since its Victorian and Edwardian heyday. All but a handful of the mills are silent, many demolished, but, having hit rock bottom, Bradford is bouncing back, as the council slogan tells you.

In 1985 the City's football ground was the scene of an horrific disaster, which is etched deep into the memory of the people of Bradford, but that disaster also revealed their resilience, character and community spirit, traits much in evidence in the next classic town pub, the Cock & Bottle.

Approach it from Forster Square in the heart of the city, taking the road up past the cathedral, partly obscured by the old General Post Office, now the offices of an insurance company. The Cock & Bottle stands a few yards past the cathedral at the side of the city's new inner ring road. A tunnel connects the pub to the cathedral and there is a local legend that Lady Fairfax was chased into the cathedral during the Civil War and captured as she tried to make her escape from the pub.

The Cock & Bottle is another of Tetley's Heritage Inns and is a magnificent example of a Victorian public house, with fine ceilings, beautiful mahogany fittings and superb, stained, etched and engraved glass. There is a separate entrance to the taproom, which has fine, partitioned bench seats and a cast-iron fireplace. This room was featured in the Albert Finney/Tom Courtenay film *The Dresser*.

There is a lovely main bar with two tiny snugs off it, and at the back of the pub is the music room. A juke box provides music part of the time, but Friday night is cabaret night, and on Saturday night and Sunday lunchtime a pianist provides accompaniment to anyone who wants to get up and sing. What the singers may lack in talent and technique they more than make up for in sheer enjoyment and enthusiasm; even the worst bring pleasure to at least two people – the singer and the landlord, who

The Cock & Bottle
Licensees: Terri & Roni Breakwell
93 Barkerend Road, Bradford
☎ Bradford (0274) 722403
11 - 3; 5.30 - 11

Tetley Mild, Bitter

Lunchtime food. Families welcome at lunchtime. Outside drinking area.

The Cock & Bottle, Bradford – the wool merchants are all but gone; the pub remains a classic

profits from the rush to the bar to get away from the sound!

Around the front of the bar are cupboards that were once used by the city's wool merchants. The merchants would deposit their wool samples in them before rounding-up likely purchasers, who would be brought up to the Cock & Bottle to be plied with drink in the hope of a favourable response to the samples. If the beer was as good as the magnificent Tetleys the Cock & Bottle serves today, one can begin to see why so much wool was bought and sold in Bradford!

There are three versions of the origin of the pub name. One says that it is named for the beer cock used to dispense beer; another, that it refers to a haycock and the wickerwork framework known as a 'bottle' that was used to allow air to circulate inside the haycock to stop it from rotting; and the third, that it was named because of cock-fights that took place there.

The Cock & Bottle is a superb example of Victorian opulence, but the clientele puts on no airs and graces. You will find city gents rubbing shoulders with rag-and-bone men and a pub atmosphere which, in its warmth, character and earthiness, reflects the city which it serves so well.

Bradford is also home to the very successful Fighting Cocks chain of back-to-basics pubs. The first was the Fighting Cock in Preston Street, once looking out over an ocean of industrial decay, now handily placed for the vast new development of the Grattan mail order company. Drive out along Thornton Road from the city centre and you will find Preston Street about half a mile on your left, just before the Grattan complex.

The Fighting Cock has bare boards, lived-in furnishings, peeling paint and an outside Gents, but what brings people to it is (obviously) not the decor, but its bewildering range of beers, its atmosphere and 'the crack'. It is the archetypal basic boozer and, along with the other members of the Fighting Cocks chain, it is doing well on its simple but highly successful formula.

Plenty of other pubs have tried to offer as wide a range of beers, but most have failed to keep them in such good condition. Choose one of the many guest beers listed on the blackboard hung over the big stone fireplace, where a blazing open fire greets winter customers, or drink one of the regular beers in the company of the Fighting Cock's many regular customers; the quality of the beer explains the quantity of the customers.

No student of our industrial heritage should leave the Bradford area without visiting Titus

The Fighting Cock
Licensee: Jim Wright
Preston Street,
Bradford
☎ Bradford (0274) 726907

Draught Bass; Boddingtons Bitter; Old Mill Traditional Bitter; Taylor Landlord; Tetley Bitter; Guest beers

Salt's remarkable model village, Saltaire, three miles from Bradford towards Keighley, just off the A650. The village was built to house the workers at Salt's massive mill, the largest in Europe, in the nineteenth-century.

Salt's paternalistic rule would not be to today's taste for the lives of his workers were certainly dominated by the decrees of the mill owner, but, compared to the appalling conditions endured by the majority of Bradford and British workers in the nineteenth-century, Salt's village of solid stone houses, parks, library, hospital and almshouses, is a model of housing provision. There was only one flaw in Salt's vision, he was a teetotaller and would allow no licensed

The Fighting Cock, Bradford – no frills, no fuss, no better kept beer than here

premises in his village. As a result, the road facing onto Saltaire once boasted more pubs per square inch than anywhere else in Britain, though most have now disappeared in road-widening schemes!

One other Bradford landmark is worthy of note – Lister's Mill chimney – visible from throughout the area and so large, as any proud Bradfordian will tell you, that you could drive a carriage and four around the top . . . if you could find a way of getting them up there in the first place.

Visitors with literary interests will also want to make the pilgrimage to the nearby Brontë village of Haworth; those with less exalted spirits will wish to make the acquaintance of Timothy Taylor's Landlord, brewed in the nearby town of Keighley, and my own nominee for the finest beer in Britain. In a journey that has passed through Burton, the home of the British brewing style, what could be better than to end this part of our travels with a pint that demonstrates how good that style can still be in the right hands – no adjuncts, no additives, no advertising hype, just a magnificent pint of beer?

THE GREAT
NORTH ROAD

The Great North Road has been one of the main arteries of Britain since Roman times. It follows the line of the Roman Ermine Street for much of its length, connecting the English and Scottish capitals with the major commercial centres of pre-industrial Britain, and was at its peak in the turnpike age, when hundreds of coaches a day travelled north and south along it. Many of the inns we shall visit served the coaching trade, though several pre-date it by hundreds of years.

With the Industrial Revolution, the focus of Britain's wealth shifted west and north, away from the rich agricultural lands of the eastern plains, towards the expanding cities we have already visited. The railways took much of the traffic that had once used the Great North Road, and when the motorway age came, it was the M6 and the M1 that became the main routes to the north. The all but forgotten A1 has now enjoyed something of a revival, appealing to motorists who cannot stomach the motorway mania of the M1, but it has been so heavily improved, with the towns and cities it once connected all by-passed, that there is scarcely a section of the road where you are travelling along its original line.

It is possible to drive from London to Edinburgh without doing more than glimpse a town, but that way you will get no understanding of the country you travel through. Turn off and visit some of our most historic and beautiful towns, and call at some of our finest pubs as well. I have given directions from the present A1, but one unexpected benefit of the improvements that have been made to it is that for much of its length the old Great North Road survives as an excellent, and little used A or B road running parallel to the A1. If you are in no great hurry, the journey will be much less stressful that way.

The first stop is at Stamford, well north of where the stagecoach passengers would have paused for refreshment two centuries ago, but the wait is well worth it, for the pub is a magnificent survival from that coaching age in a town that has remained virtually unaltered since then.

Turn off the A1 towards Stamford and pass by the magnificent gatehouse to Burghley House, home of the Cecils and host to the annual Burghley Horse Trials. Drive down Stamford's delightful St Martins, the main road leading through the town, and you cannot miss the George, for its 'gallows' sign – one of very few left in England, for most were removed as a danger to traffic – arches over the road ahead of you.

Previous page: The nautical memorabilia in the Minerva at Hull are a link to the days when the quayside was alive with passengers and cargo

The George
Licensee: Philip Newman-Hall
71 St Martins,
Stamford,
Lincolnshire
☎ Stamford (0780) 55171
11 - 2.30; 6 - 11

No real ale

Lunchtime & evening food. Restaurant. Accommodation. Families welcome. Garden.

The George was built in 1597 for Lord Burghley, but it stands on the site of the House of the Holy Sepulchre, a monastic hospice where the Knights of St John of Jerusalem were entertained at the time of the Crusades. Charles I stayed there on several occasions, the last time in 1645, when, disguised as a servant, he fled from Oxford and spent the night in Stamford, his last as a free man, before joining the Scottish army at Newark. He was handed over to Cromwell by the Scots and remained under arrest until his trial and execution.

Danial Lambert, the most obese man in English history, in residence at the George, Stamford

At either side of the stone-flagged hall of the George are the London and York rooms, named for the destination of the coaches that stopped there in the turnpike age. Over forty coaches a day paused for refreshment and a change of horses at the George and, though the Great North Road now by-passes Stamford, many people still find their way to the town and its famous inn.

The London Room is a magnificently panelled restaurant. The York Room, also panelled, contains the George's only disappointment – a bar without real ale. That such a superb traditional inn should not serve traditional ale is an aberration that I hope the George will rectify before too long.

There is a splendidly polished brass shoe-shine stand in the hall, where you may sit in the hope, probably forlorn, that some lackey may appear and polish your boots. The lounge contains a superb fireplace with stone recesses to either side and at the back of the George is a courtyard area, part-covered, where you can eat or drink surrounded by trees and ivy-covered walls with the addition of flower tubs and hanging baskets in summer. You can improve your chess on a king-size board in the courtyard and there is also a walled garden with a sunken lawn on which you may be able to try out your croquet technique. The gnarled, old mulberry bush dates from the reign of James I.

Eat in the courtyard or in the sub-tropical Garden Lounge surrounded by banks of banana trees, creepers and flowers. The menu changes with the seasons, making much use of fresh, local ingredients and it is good enough to put you in mind of a famous person with Stamford connections, Daniel Lambert, who has a room at the George named in his honour.

Mr Lambert's singular achievement was to be the most enormous man in England. He weighed in at about eight pounds in 1770 and weighed out at fifty-two stone eleven pounds in 1809. Whether his obesity was glandular or dietary, history does not relate, but go easy on the puddings, just in case.

Before leaving Stamford, take a stroll across

the bridge over the Welland with ducks nestling in the grass at the water's edge. Do not be tempted to 'skinny dip' though, as a bye-law states that 'every person above the age of twelve years who shall bathe in the River Welland, or any other river, brook or open water or indecently expose his person within eighty yards of any dwelling-house or of any public foot or carriage way within the liberties of the said Borough, shall forfeit and pay any sum not exceeding ten shillings.'

Stamford was founded by the Danes in 700 and grew rich on the medieval wool trade. Though almost destroyed during the Wars of the Roses, it revived and prospered as the Great North Road grew in importance, and, though the road has moved on, the town continues to thrive. See the fine St Mary's Church, count the antique shops, if you can, then follow the main street north as it leads you away from the old Great North Road and back to the brash, modern A1.

The huge inglenook at the Angel & Royal, Grantham

In coaching days, the next halt after Stamford for a stagecoach going north was at Grantham. We, too, will stop there at another magnificent old inn, the Angel & Royal, which stands at the north end of the High Street. It is yet another of England's myriad 'oldest inns' and, like the George at Stamford, it found early use as a hospice for Crusaders – the Knights Templar.

The superb stone facade is covered in carvings and gargoyles, though many of them are so weathered as to be almost unrecognizable. Above the great archway is one that reflects the inn's name, an angel holding a crown, and to either side of the arch are carvings of King Edward III and his Queen Philippa, erected when they visited the inn during the fourteenth century. The central oriel window was also constructed to commemorate the visit.

Edward III was one of many royal visitors, though it is doubtful if another, Richard III, enjoyed his visit quite as much. While staying in the inn's ancient Chambre du Roi (now the restaurant) in 1483, he wrote to the Lord Chancellor in London, asking for the Great Seal to be sent so that he could sign the death warrant of the treacherous Duke of Buckingham. The original of the letter is in the British Museum, but a copy hangs in the Angel & Royal. King John, the unwilling father of British democracy, also visited the inn in 1209 and 1213. In 1866, Edward VII, then the Prince of Wales, visited the inn and his stay occasioned the change of name from the original 'Angel' to the 'Angel & Royal'. The name 'The Royal Angel' was suggested, but as Edward was certainly no angel, the present

The Angel & Royal
Manager: Peter G Willcock
High Street,
Grantham,
Lincolnshire
☎ Grantham (0476) 65816
11 - 3; 6 - 11

Adnams Bitter; Draught Bass; Greene King Abbot

Lunchtime & evening food. Restaurant. Accommodation. Courtyard. Families welcome.

The unique 'living' sign at the Beehive, Grantham

name was felt to be more appropriate!

The Falcon bar, to one side of the great arch, has a fine, timbered ceiling, a stone fireplace and a lovely stone-vaulted window. The Angel bar, on the other side, has a massive inglenook, more beams and an even lovelier window, with a fine wooden carving below it. On the first floor is the King's Room restaurant, with a spiral staircase in one corner leading up to a vantage point once manned by the royal look-out. Tunnels reputedly led from the cellar beneath the inn to the Market Square and to St Wulfram's church, which has the sixth tallest spire in England and is a notable landmark for miles around.

There is a set of stocks in the courtyard, where on fine days, you can sit at tables to reflect on the Angel & Royal's remarkable history. Grantham, itself, has many points of greater or lesser historical significance too. It was voted Britain's 'most boring town' in a radio poll a few years ago, but of more interest may be the fact that Isaac Newton was educated at the Kings School; a huge bronze statue of the great man stands in St Peter's Hill and his name is inscribed on a window sill of the Old School House. Margaret Thatcher is another famous Grantham scientist, though her career has yet to be crowned with a similar statue in her home town.

One other sight worth seeing can be found at the Beehive Inn in Castlegate. The pub sign hangs in a lime tree outside the pub and is unique – a beehive full of real bees! Leaving Grantham you cross that rarity in the east of England,

The award-winning Wig & Mitre at Lincoln proves that pubs don't have to be long-established to be excellent

a hill, giving magnificent views over the massive plain to the North as you once more rejoin the A1.

The next few classic pubs lead us away from the Great North Road. We will re-join it beyond York, but for now, our course runs to the east of it. If you are in a hurry, follow the A1 north to Newark then turn east onto the A46, the Roman Fosse Way. If you would prefer a slower and more restful road, take the A607 from Grantham, leading north to Lincoln.

Lincoln cathedral is a majestic sight, visible from a long way off, for it and the castle sit on a hill rising two hundred feet above the surrounding plains. The heart of the city is one of the most historic in England, and it is often thronged with tourists as a result. The castle dates from 1068, when William the Conqueror ordered its construction, the cathedral from 1072, though, after a fire in 1141 and an earthquake in 1185, work on the present building began in 1192 and was completed in 1311.

The cathedral is the third largest in England and is full of interest, from the original west facade, the bell known as 'Great Tom of Lincoln', which weighs over five tons, and the Angel Choir to the Lincoln Imp carved at its eastern end. The massive western gatehouse of the Cathedral Close faces the castle down Exchequer Gate.

A thousand years before the coming of the Normans, Lincoln was a major Roman town, *Lindum*, at the intersection of two great roads, the Fosse Way and Ermine Street. There have been several excavations, revealing parts of the walls and streets and the Roman East Gate.

Lincoln, like Stamford, grew wealthy on the wool trade in the Middle Ages, and there is much to see in addition to the castle, the magnificent cathedral and the Roman remains. Steep Hill is the route followed by medieval pilgrims to the cathedral and it leads down to the twelfth-century Jews Quarter, containing what is said to be the oldest inhabited house in England. Steep Hill also contains the Wig & Mitre, where you may well want to stop and have a drink and a bite to eat.

The Wig & Mitre was a derelict antique shop which was restored as a pub in 1977 with such care that it won a national award. Many of the fourteenth-century timbers were used in the reconstruction and sections of the original lime, ash and reed floor have been retained above the first floor bar and restaurant to illustrate medieval building techniques. The upstairs area has a large stone fire-

The Wig & Mitre – an excellent pub in one of Britain's most historic cities

place, a bar with a curved bench seat and a shelf full of books for those who want to relax and read. The day's newspapers are also available, or you can look out at the bustle of Steep Hill from the comfortable alcoved seats of the downstairs bar. To one side is a small terrace area with clematis and Russian vine growing over a trellis.

If all this sounds good enough, what makes the Wig & Mitre particularly special is the thought, care and attention to detail which the owners, Michael and Valerie Hope, have put into it. The philosophy of many publicans is often to be found between the racing pages of the Sun, and the number of people who have gone into the licensed trade with only the vaguest of notions as to what they are doing there and why is astounding. The result is a large number of sour-faced Basil Fawltys behind the bars of Britain, who have realized too late what the job actually entails, and are determined to take out their resentment on their hapless customers.

The owners of the Wig & Mitre, however, have set out to create the sort of pub where the customer is always the most important person in the place. There are no electronic games, no muzak and no smell of chips frying, so it is a real pleasure to spend time in. And time is something there is always plenty of in the Wig & Mitre, because another of the Hopes' excellent innovations has been to open from eight in the morning to midnight.

You can eat a very good breakfast and stay for morning coffee, lunch, afternoon tea and dinner too, if you have a mind to. You can also eat breakfast at ten at night or dinner at breakfast time – another example of the Hopes' desire to please the customer. The licensing laws still impose some restriction, of course, but you can take an afternoon drink in the restaurant or have a tea, coffee or soft drink while waiting for Lloyd George's idea of a proper time to drink to come round.

Prices are reasonable, the wine list is good, and, best of all, it is neither an American bar nor a continental-style brasserie; it retains all the atmosphere of a proper British pub, a worthy complement to an historic city.

From Lincoln, Ermine Street runs straight as an arrow towards the north; follow it, as it takes us towards the Humber and the city of Hull. The country north of Lincoln is another of England's little-known and little-visited areas, with an elaborate gateway or lodge to some vast estate every few miles. As in most of East Anglia, hedges are very scarce commodities, so the horizons are significantly extended by the few feet of height gained where parts of

The Wig & Mitre
Licensees: Michael & Valerie Hope
29 Steep Hill,
Lincoln
☎ Lincoln (0522) 35190/ 23705
8am until midnight every day

Samuel Smith Old Brewery Bitter, Museum Ale

Lunchtime & evening food. Restaurant. Families welcome. Patio.

the road run along embankments set above the surrounding wetlands.

Pass through Redbourn with its unusual sign warning of ducks crossing the road, and through Brigg, a pleasant town with a wealth of inns that signifies its importance as a coaching stop, the first on the journey south from Hull. In a good year the rich farmland is laden with corn, barley, sugar beet and potatoes. Here, as elsewhere, the fields were also once full of poppies, wild oats and flowering herbs as well as the main crop, but these so-called weeds have long since been banished – another triumph for the chemical industry! They survive in the roadside verges, unpoisoned by anything but the fumes of the internal combustion engine.

The A15 towards Hull continues to follow the line of the Roman Ermine Street. What the Romans would have made of the twentieth-century engineering wonder, the Humber Bridge, which is the longest single-span suspension bridge in the world, is an interesting speculation. I am sure they would have been impressed; so will you when you've stumped up the hefty toll for the crossing over the Humber.

Hull, in common with many British ports, is but a shadow of the thriving city it was. Virtually no fish is landed there now and its cargo traffic is a fraction of that handled in its heyday, but the city and its inhabitants retain their Yorkshire character and independence. The biting cold of the wind howling in off the North Sea is at least partly offset by the warmth of the Hull people!

Those who shudder at the memory of Hull, one-third of the infamous 'Hull, Hell and Halifax' of the ancient ballad, will be pleasantly surprised by the Old Town, containing one of the finest medieval high streets in England, and two classic town pubs as well. The first pub provides a link to one of Hull's most famous native sons, William Wilberforce, who did more than anyone to outlaw the slave trade from England.

The leaded windows of the Black Boy look out onto the narrow winding High Street as they have done since at least 1331, when the inn was first mentioned. It has been by turns a corn merchants, a private residence, a wines and spirits merchants, a gin shop, a brothel, a coffee shop, and a tobacco and snuff shop and has now settled for the role of an excellent pub. A corridor leads to the dark-panelled front bar with a carving of a black boy over the fireplace and to the public bar at the back, where you can enjoy a band playing traditional folk music every Sunday lunchtime. The walls are decorated with handbills and prints about the slave trade, reflecting the pub name

Opposite: Ye Olde Black Boy, Hull, commemorates both the slave trade and the Hull man who outlawed it from Britain

Ye Olde Black Boy
Licensee: Charles Orr
High Street,
Hull,
Humberside
☎ Hull (0482) 26516
11 - 3.30; 5.30 - 10.30 (11 Friday and Saturday)

Tetley Mild, Bitter

Lunchtime & evening food. Families welcome.

and the Wilberforce connection. Upstairs are two further rooms, each with fine, carved and moulded fireplaces.

Two tunnels once led from beneath the floor in the front bar; one to Holy Trinity church, possibly of use during the troubles of the Civil War, and the other to the river, certainly of use to smugglers. As you would expect in a pub of its age, the Black Boy has a ghost, a man in a high hat and white pantaloon trousers.

As you would also expect, there are several variants on the origin of the pub name. One claims that it dates from the days when the tobacconist on the site used a black boy as a door boy and advertising gimmick, another that it dates from around 1730, when Carter's coffee house had a Moroccan dressed in native garb, and the last that it relates to the slave markets held in the High Street.

Another pub with strong historical links is the Olde White Hart in Silver Street. In 1642, in an upstairs room, ever since called the Plotting Parlour, the Governor of Hull, a Parliamentarian called Sir John Hotham, ordered the town gates to be closed against Charles I who was on his way from York. Charles was denied the use of the city arsenal and forced to withdraw to Beverley. This, the first major act of the Civil War, illustrates the characteristic independence of Humbersiders; even today Hull is the only city in Britain with its own private telephone system, and its own white telephone boxes!

To reach the other Hull classic pub, head past the gilded statue of King William III – 'our Great Deliverer', as the inscription tells us – down to Victoria Pier, where in the past ferries plied the Humber and the wharves were busy with cargoes that once included slaves. No cargo is landed and no ferries leave the Victoria Pier now, but the quayside is a pleasant place to sit or stroll, made even more so by the presence of another excellent pub, the Minerva.

Built in 1830, the Minerva was an important hotel, as its imposing frontage suggests. The staff were required to speak French and German, indicating the cosmopolitan nature of Hull at the time; nowadays they stick to English with a Yorkshire accent! The Minerva is also notable for being the only brewery in Hull, brewing its own Pilot's Pride ale once a week.

Enter the Minerva up a couple of steps from the quayside. The pub has recently been restored with great care and sensitivity, leaving the central, wood-panelled bar surrounded by a series of comfortable inter-linked rooms. As well as the main bar with its open fire, there is a tiny four-person snug, a food servery and a very

The Minerva
Licensees: John & Julie McCue
Nelson Street,
Hull,
Humberside
☎ Hull (0482) 26909
11 - 3.30; 6 - 10.30 (11 Friday and Saturday)

Minerva Pilot's Pride; Tetley Mild, Bitter

Lunchtime & evening food. Families welcome.

welcoming food and family area with a massive iron pillar in the centre of the room and big windows looking out across the quay. There is a darts area down a couple of steps with a cast-iron fireplace flanked by two tall cupboards and, as well as the nautical pictures that decorate the whole pub, there is a menu from an 1873 Choir dinner. The menu included mock turtle soup, calf's head hash, stewed pigeons, twelve cuts of meat and seven puddings. You won't get quite such a substantial meal at the Minerva these days, but the portions are ample enough for twentieth-century appetites!

The Victoria Pier has lost the commercial activity that made it a vital part of the life of the

The Minerva – the only brewery in Hull and a fine pub as well

City of Hull, but the Minerva remains an excel-lent pub and reason enough to visit the old docks. While there, you can also visit the Herit-age Centre and walk along the quay, looking out towards the sea or inland to the Humber Bridge, arching gracefully over the river.

Leave Hull to the north, taking the A1079 towards York, then turn off onto the A1174 to Beverley. From here Beverley is only a short distance away, and its magnificent Gothic Minster, like the other cathedrals, mins-ters and churches of the plains, dominates the view for miles around. Like Ely Cathedral in East Anglia, the size of Beverley Minster is out of proportion to the present importance of the town, evidence both of the richness of the sur-rounding agricultural land and of the commer-cial as well as religious significance of saints' relics and pilgrimages in medieval times.

The remarkable 'Nellie's' – the White Horse at Beverley

The Minster was founded as a priory around the start of the eighth-century by Bishop John of York, whose tomb stands in the nave. The original building suffered at the hands of the Danes in the ninth century and from a fire in the twelfth century; work on the present building began in 1220 and continued until 1400. As well as Bishop John's tomb, there is the superb Gothic tomb of Lady Percy and the ninth-century Fridstool, which guaranteed the safety of law-breakers who sought sanctuary.

Beverley is a delightful town and you may want to wander the main street for a while, browsing in its multitude of book and antique shops, but be sure that your wanderings eventually lead you down Hengate, just by St Mary's Church, for down there you will find the White Horse, universally known as 'Nellie's' and one of the most distinctive pubs you could hope to meet.

The sign is a model of a white horse standing above the door, and the age of the pub is obvious from the bulging old brick walls. A stone-flagged entrance hall leads into a maze of rooms, and I defy you to keep track of the number as you explore the pub! The central bar has a magnificent old cash register, bare boards and an open fire with fine inset tiles. There is no electricity, lighting is by gas, including a superb chandelier, and there are Victorian pictures and huge mirrors on the walls.

Around the bar is a corridor leading to the innumerable small rooms, all with fireplaces; to keep all Nellie's fires burning must have required the entire production of the Yorkshire

The White Horse (Nellie's)
Licensee: Bruce Westaby
Hengate,
Beverley,
Humberside
☎ Hull (0482) 861973
10.30 - 3.30 (4 Wednesday, 5 Saturday); 6 - 10.30 (11 Friday and Saturday)

Samuel Smith Old Brewery Bitter, Museum Ale

Lunchtime & evening food. Restaurant. Families welcome. Garden.

coafield! There are two superb old iron ranges, an ancient and venerable gas cooker and much else besides. At the back is a cobbled yard with wooden tables and an old well. Upstairs there are yet more rooms, including one used by the White Horse folk club, every Monday at 8.30.

The pub gets its nickname from the indomitable landlady who ran it until 1976 and it is known by her name throughout Beverley. The following two examples of her character may explain the mixture of awe, amusement and admiration she inspired. If her fruit machine paid out too much, she would be straight out to turn it off, telling the unfortunate customer that it was out of order. Her long-time live-in lover acquired the nickname 'Suitcase Johnny' from the locals because of the number of times that the irate Nellie pitched his suitcase containing his worldly goods into the street in the middle of one of their frequent arguments.

However, though very definitely a character, she was by no means the ogre that this suggests and she is fondly remembered by her customers. The pub is little altered since her day, though the bar is a recent innovation; in Nellie's time, beer was carried through from the back. Nellie may have gone, but her memory definitely lingers on in this unspoilt pub.

Leave Beverley to the west, past the rather homespun race course, and pick up the A1079 towards York. You pass through the lovely village of Bishop Burton, with its fine stone houses surrounding the green and pond. Though this is very much still the flatlands, a hill before Market Weighton gives an absolutely stunning view out over the Plain of York to the distance spires of York Minster.

York is one of the most beautiful towns in England, rich in history, fine buildings and places of interest. Its origins trace back to the Roman garrison town of *Eboracum*, which became the capital of the province of Britannia and was where emperors such as Hadrian and Constantine had their villas. In post-Roman times, it became the capital of the Saxon kingdom of Northumbria under the name of Eoforwic. Later it was conquered first by the Danes in 867, who renamed it Jorvik, and then by the Normans in 1069.

The city walls, first erected by the Normans, but mostly dating from the fourteenth century, survive in remarkable condition and a stroll along them is an ideal start to a visit to York. Each of the city gates has its stories to tell. Above Micklegate Bar, the main entrance from the south, the heads of beheaded criminals were displayed. Bootham Bar to the north, was the site of decisive battles against the Scots, while

Walmgate Bar was pounded by the artillery of Cromwell's army in the Civil War. From Monk Bar there is a superb view of the Minster, which must be on every visitor's itinerary. While Durham cathedral is the more impressive building, York Minster's medieval stained glass is one of the wonders of the world.

The original seventh-century building was destroyed by the Normans in 1069. The present building was begun in the early twelfth-century, though work was not completed until 1472. It has several times been damaged by fire, most recently in 1984, but its magnificent stained glass, notably the 'Five Sisters', has somehow survived fire, war and siege to delight visitors today.

York has a wealth of other attractions, including the Castle Museum, the National Railway Museum, the Merchant Adventurer's Hall, the Guildhall, where the English paid a vast ransom to the Scots for the release of Charles I, and Clifford's tower, the only surviving remnant of the Norman castle. Equally interesting are the medieval streets of the Shambles, and there you will find the first of York's two classic town pubs.

Stonegate, in the heart of the Shambles, is a pedestrian street and one of York's most delightful and most expensive thoroughfares. Among the chic shops, you will not miss the Olde Starre, for, like the George at Stamford, it has a 'gallows' sign stretching right across the street. Reach the Starre through a narrow alleyway, opening out into a forecourt where you can sit at the wooden tables and enjoy a magnificent view of the towers of the Minster across the rooftops of the Shambles.

Inside the pub you will find a rambling collection of rooms; a bench-seated dining-room, a children's room, a mahogany-topped cocktail bar with stained glass, wood panelling and a fine cast-iron fireplace, and a large, main bar area where tourists and locals mix happily together. The windows look out onto a walled beer garden.

The Olde Starre is one of the oldest licensed houses in York and has its share of associations with the famous and infamous and its obligatory ghosts. Dick Turpin and Guy Fawkes were both born within shouting distance and the ghosts include two black cats, and an old lady seen lying on the floor in one of the bedrooms by a previous licensee's child. Two landlords have seen their dogs knock themselves out on the pillar in the bar, when hurling themselves at some apparition invisible to human eyes.

In the cellar are more ghostly presences; some of the wounded from the siege of York

Ye Olde Starre Inne
Licensee: Gaynor Hartley
40 Stonegate,
York
☎ York (0904) 23063
11 - 3; 5.30 - 11

Cameron Lion Bitter,
Strongarm

Lunchtime food. Evening food 5.30 - 7.30 (June-September only). Families welcome. Garden.

during the Civil War were laid on the stone slabs in the cellar while having their wounds treated. This often involved the amputation of limbs without the benefits of an anaesthetic and it is claimed that on certain nights you can still hear the screams of the wounded.

William Foster, the landlord of the Olde Starre during the siege of York in 1644, was a Royalist supporter who had the misfortune to see his pub used for roisterous celebrations by the victorious Roundhead forces, an event commemorated in a contemporary piece of doggerel:

A bande of soldiers with boisterous dinne,
Filled up large kitchen of ye Olde Starre Inne.
Some rounde ye spacious chimney, smoking satt,
And whiled ye time in battle talk and chat,
Some at ye brown cake table gamed and swore,
While pikes and matchlocks strewed ye sanded floore,
Will Foster ye hoste, mid ye groupe was seene,
With full redd face, bright eye and honest miene;
He smoked in silence in his olde inn chaire,
No joke nor jestes disturbed his sadden'd air.

Many landlords share Will Foster's taciturnity with less excuse, but the present licensee is not one of them. She runs a lively, friendly pub, a welcome resting point on the tour of York's many superb tourist sights and sites.

When you have refreshed yourself, wander through the streets of the Shambles and then make your way by Petersgate, Colliergate and Stonebow to Peasholme Green, where you will find the Black Swan.

The 'gallows' sign of Ye Olde Starre Inne, York

Stonebow and Peasholme Green are not the best preserved or most attractive streets in York by a long chalk, but the Black Swan more than makes up for their shortage of charm. Forty years ago the pub had a drab plaster exterior, but restoration has revealed the superb half-timbering concealed beneath it.

The Black Swan is reputed to be York's oldest inn (as is the Olde Starre; such conflicting claims are the lifeblood of lively pub discussion and to offer irrefutable proof one way or the other would be the height of bad manners!) For many generations it was the home of the Bowes family, who number a Lord Mayor of York and a Lord Mayor of London among the branches of their family tree. When the Bowes left the house, it passed to the Thompsons, among whom was the mother of General Wolfe of Quebec.

The oak door leads into a stone-flagged entrance hall. On one side of the bar is the Oak Room, an oak-panelled room with an unusual herringbone-pattern brick fireplace and an almost invisible oil painting over it, the paint all but obscured by centuries of smoke from the fire and the customers' tobacco. The main bar is dominated by a massive inglenook with a spit-roast. There is a fine carved wood chair to one side of the fireplace, lots of beams and panelling and a really warm and welcoming atmosphere.

As well as the normal range of pub grub, the Black Swan offers daily specials, often including a giant Yorkshire pudding with beef stew that, together with the heat from the fire, will give you a rosy glow on even the coldest winter day.

The fine half-timbering of the Black Swan, York, was hidden for years beneath a layer of rendering

The Black Swan Inn
Licensee: Robert Burrow Atkinson
Peasholme Green, York
☎ York (0904) 25236
11 - 3; 5.30 - 11

Draught Bass; Stones Best Bitter

Lunchtime food. Evening food for party bookings only. Families welcome. Accommodation. Live jazz and folk music some nights.

Before you leave, take a look upstairs in the Wolfe Room, named in honour of his links with the city and the pub, and reached by a fine oak staircase. It is used for party bookings and for business meetings and is a quite superb Tudor room, with decorated oak-panelling, lattice-pattern leaded windows and a very unusual fireplace, lined with antique tiles.

From York take the A59 west towards Harrogate, then follow the B6265 north from Green Hammerton, along the Roman Dere Street to Boroughbridge. There you rejoin the Great North Road, running along the plains, with the hills of the Pennine Dales rising to the west and the Hambleton Hills and the Wolds far to the east.

Follow it north past Scotch Corner, an important road junction in Roman times, and the place where, as the name suggests, turnpike traffic making for Scotland turned to the west, leaving the Great North Road to those making for Durham and Newcastle, which is where we are now heading. A few miles further north, there is an abrupt transition from the farmlands of the Plain of York to the collieries of the Durham coalfield. Durham was an important town long before the coalfields began to produce their black gold, however, and it contains what is perhaps our finest Norman cathedral, in what is certainly the most spectacular setting of any in England. Cathedral and castle stand proudly, high above the town on a natural fortress site – a tongue of steep-sided land, surrounded on three sides by the sinuous River Wear.

Turn off the A1 at the Durham sign and follow the A690 down into the city, beneath the massive bulk of the cathedral, dwarfing even the castle alongside it. Drop down the hill towards the city and drive into the multi-storey car park that is signed off the roundabout. Durham city centre is definitely not user-friendly to motorists and this car park is very handy both for the cathedral and castle, and for the Durham classic town pub. Follow the cathedral and castle signs out of the car park, and you will emerge on Saddler Street. Turn left and you will see the Shakespeare Tavern just up the road on the right hand side. Shakespeare's connection with Durham is as genuine as the 'Brewers' Tudor' half-timbering on the outside of the Shakespeare, but the atmosphere inside is genuine enough.

There is a small front bar, with bench seats, Britannia tables and leaded windows. A passageway leads to a tiny snug and a cosy lounge with photographs of Durham in the 1930s on

The Shakespeare Tavern
Licensee: Anne Gloyne
Saddler Street,
Durham
☎ Durham (0385) 69709
11 - 3; 5.30 - 10.30 (No later closing at weekends)

McEwan 80/-; Younger's No 3

Food: sandwiches and toasties only, lunchtimes and evenings. Families welcome at lunchtimes.

The Shakespeare, Durham – the half-timbering here is as genuine as the Shakespearian connections!

the walls. Luxurious the Shakespeare certainly is not, but if you like homespun local pubs, then the chance to enjoy a drink, a warm welcome and the 'crack' with a mixture of regulars, students and visitors in an old-fashioned northern local will more than make up for the lack of fancy fittings and furnishings.

If you are not already aware of the fact, a few minutes in an assortment of north-east pubs will show you that they are different from their cousins elsewhere in England. They are a halfway house towards the bars we shall find in some parts of Scotland, tending to the strictly functional, with a resolutely masculine air about many of them that is less common further south. Like the Shakespeare, however, what these pubs may lack in refinements, they more than make up for with the warmth of their welcome.

When you have washed the travel dust from your throat, travel on up Saddler Street and turn right onto the stone setts of Owen Gate, which will lead you to the castle and cathedral. Durham city was founded in the tenth century by monks fleeing from Lindisfarne. It was fortified by William the Conqueror after the 'Harrying of the North' and its cathedral was constructed between 1093 and 1133 on the site of the earlier monastery. The nave of the cathedral is perhaps the finest in Europe and the cathedral contains the tombs of St Cuthbert, much visited by medieval pilgrims, and the Venerable Bede. On the superb twelfth-century portal is a doorknocker of a grotesque face with an iron ring in its mouth. Criminals were guaranteed sanctuary if they laid a hand on the ring before their pursuers laid hands on them.

The castle, facing the cathedral on the rocky heights above the Wear, was the base of the 'Prince Bishops' of Durham, whose influence extended from Durham to Scotland. Its Norman gatehouse is unique in Britain. Durham is also notable for being the site of the third oldest university in Britain, after Oxford and Cambridge, and since 1832 the castle has acted as the university's main building.

From Durham the route is north once more, to the other great city of the North-East, Newcastle upon Tyne, our last stop before the Scottish border. Crossing the River Tyne from Gateshead, Newcastle is an imposing sight. Like most British towns, it has its share of post-war excrescences, but the heart of the city is cosmopolitan and lively. The silhouette of the Tyne Bridge, is Newcastle's universally recognizable emblem, familiar to drinkers from the labels of the town's eponymous brown ale. The Black Gate of the castle houses the only bagpipe museum in the world – a raid from over the border to reclaim this vital part of Scotland's heritage seems inevitable!

Newcastle's classic town pub sits in the shadow of the massive Tyne Bridge on a street called, simply, Side, which leads, as the name suggests, down to the quayside. Once a thriving port full of ships from around the world, Newcastle is now almost a ghost port with only the occasional ship to disturb the grubby waters of the Tyne.

The uniquely named Crown Posada dates back over 220 years and had a thriving trade from Newcastle's nineteenth-century heyday but, like all good town pubs, it has adapted and survived to serve a new generation of customers. You are much more likely to encounter an advertising executive than an old salt in there these days, but the pub attracts a remarkable range of customers united in their liking for good beer and a classic town pub in which to enjoy it. If the customers have changed, the Crown Posada is virtually unaltered since the nineteenth century, and the care with which it has been preserved has won it several awards.

Enter the Crown Posada through a wrought-iron gate from the street, stepping into a long, narrow, room, divided by mahogany and stained glass screens into three areas: a small snug at the front, a narrow and incredibly busy bare-boarded area alongside the bar and a carpeted, bench-seated lounge area at the rear. There is a fine mahogany gantry at the back of the bar, an ornately moulded ceiling and some

The Crown Posada
Licensee: Mrs Christine Oldham
31 Side,
Newcastle upon Tyne
☎ Tyneside (091) 2321269
11 - 3; 5.30 - 10.30

Big Lamp Bitter; Stones Best Bitter; Taylor Landlord; Regular guest beers

Lunchtime food (sandwiches only).

The Crown Posada – the finest resting place in Newcastle named for a nineteenth-century owner's Spanish wife

lovely stained glass screens, but the pub's glory are the two superb stained glass windows, through which sunlight streams on the rare occasions that it penetrates the steep and cavernous Side. One of the windows portrays a depressed-looking pre-Raphaelite woman filling a glass, the other a rather more contented man raising his glass with some relish – it is still a man's world!

The Crown Posada got its name from a nineteenth-century owner, a sea captain, who had a wife in Spain and a mistress whom he installed at the Crown as it was then called. He changed the name to the Crown Posada because Posada is Spanish for inn or resting place. His wife may have been in Spain but his resting place was on Tyneside.

Just down Side from the pub is the Side Gallery, one of the best photographic galleries in Britain. It is also worth a wander down onto the quayside itself, where you will be dwarfed by the Tyne Bridge towering above you. On Sunday mornings there is a market on the quayside, where you may pass a pleasant hour or two while waiting for opening time. Newcastle also plays host to the biggest travelling fair in Europe – the Hoppings on the Town Moor, which takes place in mid-June each year.

Driving north from Newcastle the Northumberland landscape is gaunt and uncompromising, defying the wind whipping in from the North Sea. The multitude of castles and fortified farms show that by no means all of Northumberland's past problems have been caused by the weather. The ravages of Vikings and Scots raiders have not destroyed the region's attractions, however. There are miles of sandy beaches with scarcely a person to be seen, historic buildings and magnificent castles. Visit Alnwick, a mile or so west of the A1, and Bamburgh, which requires a detour to the coast but has one of the great castles of England.

The jewel of Northumberland is undoubtedly Holy Island, with the ruins of Lindisfarne Priory, founded in 635 and sacked by both the Danes and the Vikings. As you drive up the A1 after Bamburgh, the ruins of the twelfth-century Priory building are visible out to sea together with the fortified fourteenth-century monastery and the sixteenth-century Lindisfarne castle. If you wish, take a detour and drive out across the causeway, which is flooded at high tide, or take a boat cruise around the Farne Islands, a haven for thousands of seabirds.

Turn off the A1 at the first sign to Berwick, drop down through Tweedmouth and cross the Tweed by the fine stone viaduct, with the even more magnificent railway viaduct to the left.

The Free Trade is to the north of the town on the road back to the A1 and Edinburgh; either look round the town, its castle and fortifications first, or go and park and have a drink at the Free Trade before exploring this historic part of Britain.

Berwick played somewhat the same role in British history as Poland did in Europe; it was fought over and besieged more times than the weary inhabitants could count, as the Scots and English battled for control. Between 1147 and 1182 it changed hands no less than thirteen times, and it continued to be raided and overrun, though with less frequency, until the eighteenth-century. The town fortifications are Elizabethan, built between about 1558 and 1570 inside the thirteenth-century town walls. There are four bastions with walls over ten feet thick, built strong enough to withstand bombardment by cannons. The parish church is one of just two in Britain built during Cromwell's Republic.

It would be fair to say that the north-east of England and much of Scotland is less than blessed with the sort of outstanding pubs or, indeed, the traditional beers that make a trip through many other parts of the kingdom such a delight. However, there are still enough pubs of character to make a stop worthwhile. The Free Trade in Berwick, like the Shakespeare in Durham, is by no means a five-star drinking establishment, but it is an example of the sort of town pub that has all but disappeared elsewhere, and it has an atmosphere that encourages the practice of the dying art of conversation. If you have a donkey with an excess of hind legs, the Free Trade has a landlord who may be able to help with the problem!

The Free Trade is an old-fashioned corridor pub; the rooms open off a corridor that is not completely enclosed, but screens the front bar from patrons heading for what was once the smoke room and is now the pool room at the back. Corridor pubs were once widespread, as Victorian preference for private or semi-private drinking began to assert itself; most have been converted into open-plan drinking areas, but this one survives, virtually untouched.

The front bar has stained glass windows and a fireplace that would look better without the modern gas fire in front of it. There is a dartboard, bench seats and, horror of horrors, a TV, though Eddie swears it is only turned on for major sporting events. The television set is the bane of pubs, and they are particularly prevalent in the North-East and Scotland. They demand attention and stifle conversation, being just as distracting with the sound turned down for the flickering image keeps on drawing the eye to-

Character and atmosphere can make the most modest of pubs a classic – the Free Trade, Berwick upon Tweed

The Free Trade
Licensees: Eddie & Brenda Collins
Castlegate,
Berwick upon Tweed,
Northumberland
☎ Berwick (0289) 306498
11 - 3; 6 - 11

Lorimers Best Scotch

Families welcome.

Last stop before Scotland – the Free Trade, Berwick

wards it like a magnet. They should all be collected and sunk off the Farne Islands!

The back room at the Free Trade is where
you will find the local pool hustlers, shooting
pool and playing the juke box. Stick to the front
bar, with its rich patina of age and nicotine over-
laying its wood-grain paint, a room preserved in
sepia tones and a reminder of how atmosphere
and character can turn even the most unpretentious pub into a pleasant experience.

As you drive north from Berwick, the road
returns constantly to the coast, giving
fine views of the grey slate-like surface of
the cold North Sea. Though you are now in
'Bonnie Scotland', when you reach Torness any
Kenneth McKellar-inspired tartan notions will
be quickly and rudely shattered by the ugliness
of the nuclear power station, and as soon as you
put that behind you there is an equally ugly
cement works looming up. Restore your faith in
Scotland by turning off into Dunbar, a picturesque town with the White Sands south of the
town. If you are brave enough to cope with the
rigours of the North Sea, have a swim!

From here the A1 runs inland to Edinburgh,
the skyline dominated by Arthur's seat. If you
want to follow the coast, turn off into North
Berwick, and drive along the edge of the Firth of
Forth past Prestonpans, another of the innumerable battle sites of the warring Scots and
English.

When you reach Edinburgh, you will arrive
in the swirling mass of moving humanity and
stationary vehicles that is Princes Street. Park
the car and use your feet, the ubiquitous taxis or
buses to explore 'Auld Reekie' – your car is not
worth the bother. If you arrive in August you
may notice that there is something called the
Edinburgh Festival going on. This will make
your visit even more memorable, but will make
parking, eating, drinking and, indeed, sleeping,
much more difficult than normal.

EDINBURGH, THE HIGHLANDS, GLASGOW & BELFAST

Edinburgh is the most handsome large city in Britain. One reason for this is that the south side of Princes Street has not been developed with multi-storey shops and car parks, so the heart of the city has a wonderful air of space and light. Halfway along Princes Street is what appears to be a mock-Gothic spacecraft, actually the monument to Sir Walter Scott, but the great sight is the castle high above on Castle Rock. The Romans built a fortified camp there and its strategic importance was recognized by Scottish – and English – kings down the ages. At the highest point of the castle stands St Margaret's Chapel, the oldest building in Edinburgh, dating from 1090. At about this time the High Street, 'the Royal Mile', was laid out as a market.

Despite its growing importance, Edinburgh did not replace Perth as the Scottish capital until 1437, with work on Holyrood Palace beginning in the early sixteenth century. In 1760, Nor' Loch at the foot of the Castle Rock was drained and work began on the New Town.

To mention all the possible attractions in Edinburgh would come close to filling a book on its own; I will point you in the direction of four excellent pubs, but for the other cultural attractions, either buy a guide book or ask a policeman!

The four Edinburgh classic pubs provide a total contrast, demonstrating clearly the diversity encompassed by the word 'pub'. The first, Bennet's Bar, is on the way to the elegant and ever so slightly snooty area of Morningside. If Bennet's Bar had similar airs and graces to some of Morningside's more refined inhabitants, it would be entirely understandable, for it is an absolutely stunning bar, but it is simply a marvellous place to enjoy a drink in superb surroundings.

From the fine stained glass doors and windows that greet you as you approach the pub, to the magnificence of the interior, Bennet's is a joy to behold. A wooden bar runs the length of the room, with a lovely wooden gantry, (the Scots word for the back bar fitting) complete with old spirits barrels. Above the bench seats down the other side of the room are a series of mirrors with carved wood surrounds and inset tiled murals of ancient heroes. Indulgent cherubs gaze down from around the curved mirror tops. The ceiling is ornately moulded, and the only slightly jarring note is the gas fire in what is otherwise a handsome fireplace. The bar tables all have different maps of 'Auld Reekie' on top of them beneath sheets of glass, so you can ponder the mysteries of how to find the other classic pubs on your calling list while enjoying Bennet's

The palatial interior of Bennet's Bar, Edinburgh

Previous page: The Firth of Forth seen from the Starbank, Edinburgh

Bennet's Bar
Licensee: David Wilson
8 Levens Street,
Edinburgh
☎ Edinburgh (031) 229 5143
11 - 11 (midnight Thursday, Friday & Saturday). Sunday 12.30 - 2.30; 6.30 - 11

McEwan 70/-, 80/-

Lunchtime food. Families welcome in saloon at lunchtimes.

atmosphere and ambience.

There is also a modern saloon bar, which is pleasant and comfortable enough, but in view of the magnificence of the front bar, only the most densely packed crowds should persuade you to forsake it. When you do, it is for something completely different . . . Travel back towards the heart of the city, driving or walking along to the Royal Mile, one of the finest and most visited parts of this beautiful city. Wander around the area for a while absorbing some of its flavour, then slip down Niddry Street, across the Royal Mile and immediately east from the top of North Bridge. Niddry Street is a steeply cobbled street dropping down into Cowgate, along which cattle were once taken to market. At the bottom is an excellent pub, though very different from its elegant predecessor.

Bannerman's Bar, Edinburgh – rejuvenated in 1980, this is a brash and bonnie boozer burrowing beneath the Royal Mile

Bannerman's Bar is a basic and boisterous boozer in a group of cellars far below the level of the Royal Mile. Built in the 1770s, it was originally a port cellar and oyster bar and was visited by Robert Louis Stevenson. More recently it has been a dwelling house and a bleach workshop, before being put back into use as licensed premises in 1980. Bannerman's is stone-flagged and stone-walled with plain wooden tables or barrels, pine benches and a motley collection of chairs. There are stone fireplaces, a solid wood bar and a fine mahogany gantry. Off the main bar is a narrow, arched room and an arched back room with several oak hogsheads (54-gallon barrels) against the walls.

Despite, or perhaps because of its simplicity, Bannerman's has plenty of atmosphere and is very popular with students, tourists and locals alike. There is a good selection of malt whiskies and imported Belgian beers to complement the home-grown beer range and you can enliven your evening there with live music that ranges from jazz on Sunday through blues/jazz on Monday to traditional folk on Tuesday and Wednesday.

If you are really in the mood for music, walk along the Cowgate to the Grassmarket, turning right up Victoria Street where you will find the Preservation Hall near the top on your right. It is jam-packed every night, the clientele is young (or young at heart) and the music is loud, all of which makes for a lively night out. If your taste is for something a little less frenetic, there is another pub which is, in its own way, the equal of Bennet's. To reach it, go over North Bridge, turn left onto Princes Street, cross over and walk up into St Andrews Square. As you enter the square, turn right to find the Cafe Royal, where a three-dimensional lobster above the sign lets you know that sea-food is on the menu.

Bannerman's Bar
Licensee: Douglas Smith
212 Cowgate
Edinburgh
☎ Edinburgh (031) 556 3254
11 - midnight Monday - Thursday & Saturday. Friday 11 - 1am. Sunday 12.30 - 2.30; 6.30 - 11

Archibald Arrol's 70/-, 80/-; Caledonian Brewery 80/-, Caledonian Stout; Ind Coope Burton Ale; Guest beers

Lunchtime meals & snacks. Evenings, rolls and toasted sandwiches. Families welcome. Live music Sunday to Wednesday.

The Cafe Royal, Edinburgh – the quality of the food matches that of the decor

The Cafe Royal is another magnificent example of late-Victorian decor. You step into a marble-floored room with a large central bar. Around the outside of the room are semi-circular, leather bench seats, breaking the space into a series of more intimate areas. There is a very ornate ceiling and six tiled murals depicting famous inventors and innovators: Benjamin Franklin, William Caxton, James Watt, George Stephenson, Robert Peel and Michael Faraday. There is a magnificent mahogany gantry behind the bar and a lovely fireplace, inlaid with old tiles.

Etched glass doors lead to the Oyster Bar, where you can choose from a selection of fish and seafood dishes in surroundings that are every bit as magnificent as the bar. Fresh flowers and crisp, white linen tablecloths cover the tables, the walls are wood-panelled and there are more tiled murals and a series of stained glass windows illustrating gentlemanly sports and pastimes: archery, stalking, hunting, tennis, cricket and rugby.

The next Edinburgh classic pub would be worth a visit for its view over the Firth of Forth even if the pub was terrible, but in fact the pub is a beauty too. It also sells one of Scotland's few really bitter beers and a wide range of English ones too, so those who find Scottish brews a bit sweet for their palate can remind themselves of what they are missing from south of the border. The only problem is

The Cafe Royal
Licensee: Robert King-Clark
17 West Register Street, Edinburgh
☎ Edinburgh (031) 556 1884
11 - 11 (midnight Friday & Saturday). Sunday 7 - midnight

McEwan 70/-, 80/-; Younger's No 3

Lunchtime & evening food in Oyster Bar. Lunchtime bar snacks.

The Starbank, Edinburgh – though the advertising material is old-fashioned, the prices are right up to date!

that the price list seems to have been imported from an expensive part of southern England along with the beer!

To reach the Starbank, head west from St Andrews Square to Hanover Street, turn right, and at the bottom turn right and then first left. At the end of that road, turn right then left onto Craighall Road and at the bottom you should be about to drive straight into the Firth of Forth. Turn left instead and you will find the Starbank on your left.

The pub is a single, large L-shaped room though the stem of the L has very much the feel of a separate public bar. Beyond it is a light and airy lounge with an open fire, a huge mirror and a telescope through which you can study life on or across the Firth. Off the lounge is a paved courtyard where you can take your drink when the weather is fine. At the other side of the pub is a small snug where families often drink, and a restaurant with a changing daily menu, usually including sea-food and charcoal-grilled steaks.

Food is also available in the bar, usually a roast at lunchtimes or salads, herrings and mussels. In the evenings, the hot beef sandwiches in the bar are always popular. The whole drinking area is decorated with a vast collection of water jugs, trays, mirrors and other brewers' and distillers' advertising impedimenta. The pub is a beauty, full of life, good company and atmosphere and a selection of some of the best beer from north and south of the border.

When you have drunk your fill of Edinburgh's cultural and beery delights, follow the Firth west to the first roundabout, fork left and follow that road to the end where you will pick up a sign to the A90/A8. Follow that and at the junction at the top of Loriston Road, turn right down past Loriston Castle. Eventually you will reach a big roundabout, turn right and go straight on for more of Scotland's marvels, the Forth Bridges. Both the road and rail bridges are stunning examples of the engineering achievements of their respective ages.

North of the Firth you have several choices of route to the next stop in far-distant Aberdeen. You can turn right almost at once and follow the north shore of the Firth, meandering your way to Dundee via the old university town of St Andrews. You can head up the M90, either turning off for Dundee at the A91 and heading towards the Tay Bridge, or carrying on up to the M85 turning, just before Perth, and approaching Dundee from the west. Or you can forget about Dundee altogether and head straight for Perth, afterwards travelling on up to Aberdeen through Forfar on the A94. There are

The Starbank Inn
Licensee: Peter Todd
64 Laverockbank Road,
Trinity,
Edinburgh
☎ Edinburgh (031) 552 4141/2849
11 - 11 (11.30 Thursday - Saturday).
Sunday 12.30 - 2.30;
6.30 - 11

Belhaven 60/-, 70/-, 80/-, 90/-; Timothy Taylor Best Bitter, Landlord; Guest beers such as Samuel Smiths, Theakstons & Maclays

Lunchtime & evening food. Families welcome. Courtyard drinking area.

two things wrong with this last course of action: one is that you will miss the Tay Bridge, the other that you will also miss the home of two of Britain's most enduring institutions – breakfast marmalade and the Beano, both of which are produced in vast quantities in Dundee.

Dundee is surprisingly modern-looking on its western approaches. One expects a prim and proper old Scots lady and finds a fairly lively and vigorous sort of place instead. Dundee is jam city – the marmalade capital of the world – and the approaches to the city reveal a good deal of soft fruit being grown, much of which will doubtless find its way onto British breakfast tables, though the marmalade oranges are imported as the Tayside climate isn't that kind! Like much of Scotland, Dundee bears the scars of being fought-over down the centuries. Nothing remains of the medieval city, because the English repeatedly razed Dundee to the ground, the last time by courtesy of Cromwell's General Monck in 1651. The only fifteenth-century building to survive is St Mary's Tower and General Monck did his best to destroy that, too, having the contents of the city library piled around the base and set on fire. From Dundee Law, the highest point in the city, there is a fine view out across the Firth of Tay. The rail bridge dates from 1888, replacing one built nine years earlier, which collapsed during a storm while a train was crossing, just eighteen months after it was built.

On your way north from Dundee, you pass near to Glamis Castle, birthplace of the Queen Mother and Princess Margaret; the more famous Scottish castle with royal connections, Balmoral, lies well to the north in the heart of the Grampian Mountains. At Stonehaven, 'the gateway to Royal Deeside', the road rejoins the North Sea, last seen many miles ago, and you drive in sight of it to Aberdeen, the granite city.

The staid grey city was revitalized by the oil boom, which sent property prices soaring to London levels, but the boom was short-lived and it is now settling back into a less frenzied life. Aberdeen is a very stately looking city, with a fine skyline punctuated by a dozen or so church spires rising above the rooftops. Drive straight in on the A92, which becomes Union Street, the main street through the city. There is a beautiful stone bridge over the Dee and a very impressive approach to the city centre – even Aberdeen's lamp standards have a sense of grandeur and presence! The houses and public buildings are built from large blocks of grey granite, but despite the uniform grey the city is imposing rather than depressing, with a bit of light relief provided by the mock Gothic Town Hall, which looks pure Disneyland.

Decor in the smarter end of the Prince of Wales, Aberdeen

After such a long drive, a pub may well be your first priority and you will find an excellent one, the Prince of Wales, tucked away just behind Union Street. Turn into St Nicholas Street, by Marks & Spencers, and St Nicholas Lane is on your left. The Prince of Wales has a long main bar with bare floorboards and a bar counter running the length of the room. The bar still has a gutter along the front of it, though it is used for nothing worse than cigarette ends in these hygienic times. Pubs in Sydney, Australia, used to have a similar arrangement in the days of the 'six o'clock swill'; pray that the gutter at the Prince of Wales was never put to some of the uses the Sydney drinkers found for theirs!

At the far end of the bar is a food servery and round the corner is a stone-flagged area with carved wood and stained glass dividing the seats into booths. The main bar has a partitioned-off darts area, so there is no danger from flying missiles; there is a quiet area near the entrance, and panelled walls and pine benches in another drinking area off the bar. The Prince of Wales is very popular with the young, but like all good pubs, no one age-group dominates and there is a pleasant mix of all sorts of people of all sorts of ages.

When you have slaked your thirst, explore a little of Aberdeen. Like seemingly everywhere else in Scotland, it suffered greatly at the hands of the English, being burned to the ground by Edward III in 1337. It was reconstructed as two cities, old Aberdeen at the mouth of the Don and new Aberdeen by the Dee, and the two halves were not re-united until 1891. King's College, the Museum and Provost Skene's House are well worth seeing and there is a maze of intriguing lanes and alleys in the centre, though, like all ports, those of a more sensitive or easily embarrassed disposition may wish to avoid wandering near the docks late at night . . .

Leave Aberdeen on the Inverness Road, the A96. Once clear of the city you are soon passing through rich pasture land, suggesting at least one of the reasons why Aberdeen Angus beef is so highly prized. As you begin the climb away from the coastal plain, you pass thickly pine-forested hillsides. Climbing higher, the land itself seems to have been contoured by the wind blowing in off the sea. It is sparsely populated and the few farms are each protected by a cluster of scots pines – a sign familiar to Scots in the droving days when three scots pines meant that lodging, refreshment and grazing for their cattle were to be had at these inns scattered throughout the Scottish and English uplands.

The Prince of Wales
Licensee: Peter Birnie
St Nicholas Lane,
Aberdeen
11 - 11 (midnight Friday);
Sunday 12.30 - 2.30; 6.30 -
11

Caledonian Brewery 80/-;
Theakston Best Bitter, Old
Peculier; Younger's No 3

Lunchtime food.

A long, steady climb takes you into the mountains, where the landscape undulates softly like an ocean swell and, in late summer, the heather makes vivid purple splashes across the hillsides. Each town comes as a surprise in this vast and little-populated region, its depopulation hastened by the infamous Highland clearances, enforced in the wake of the '45 rebellion.

The road takes you past the town of Huntly, nestling in the hills of Strathbogie, with a castle that is well worth a few minutes' diversion from your route; then it is on through Keith to Elgin. This is the land of distilleries, and a happy holiday can be had touring through the Highlands and calling in to sample the wares and buy a bottle or two along the way, though both the law and common sense suggest that someone else should do the driving. You can pick up the whisky trail in Keith if you want, but you'll miss one of the best pubs in Scotland, or Britain for that matter, if you do.

Pass through Speymouth Forest and make the long descent into Fochabers, a pleasant town with a butcher claiming to produce 'world-class haggis'; since no-one makes it outside Scotland this is a bit like Americans calling their baseball championship the World Series! Cross the Spey, another of Scotland's great salmon rivers, and a long straight road soon leads you in towards Elgin with the twin stubby towers of the ruined cathedral, once one of Scotland's finest churches, away to the north. It was burnt down by Alexander Stewart, 'the Wolf of Badenoch', who also put the whole city to the torch. The supporters of John Knox and, inevitably, the troops of Cromwell, also laid waste the town.

Thunderton House is the pub you should make for in Elgin, to wash away the thoughts of all that devastation. You will find it in Thunderton Place, just off the main street through the old centre, near a remarkable parish church with a neo-classical plinth on top apparently waiting in vain for a statue to descend on it from the sky.

A great change has come over Scottish pubs in recent years: liberalisation of the Scottish licensing hours has meant that they have become infinitely more civilized places in which to drink. As a result, the pubs have become much more attractive to, and are far more widely used by, women and families, who would have given the old stand-up drink shops as wide a berth as possible.

This change towards an increasing number of families using pubs has also occurred throughout the rest of Britain, but, so far, families often exist in, at best, an uneasy truce with other pub-users. Many customers dislike hav-

The Thunderton House
Licensee: Norma Laidlaw
Thunderton Place,
Elgin,
Moray
☎ Elgin (0343) 48767
11 - 11 (12.45am Friday & Saturday); Sunday 6.30 - 11

Belhaven 80/-; Maclays 80/-; McEwan 70/-; Tennents Heeriot 80/-; Symonds Strong Vat Cider; Guest beers

Food served all day from 11 to 9.45pm. Conservatory. Specially built family room, high chairs, nappy changing facilities.

Opposite: The conservatory at Thunderton House, Elgin – opened in 1985 and one of the best pubs in Scotland

Thunderton House has a history dating back to the eleventh century and several ghosts, including that of Bonnie Prince Charlie

ing children roaming about the pub, but some publicans' idea of a family room is a draughty corridor, a flight of steps or a grotty room where only the really desperate would spend any time. The few pubs that do make a positive attempt to cater properly for families seem resigned to concentrating solely on that trade; it is as if pubs are ghettoes for only one type of customer. Yet this is a perversion of the basic strength of the pub – that it can cater harmoniously for many different kinds of customers.

It is perfectly possible to provide good facilities for families without driving away other customers, just as it is possible for a pub to serve good food without having to pollute the bars with cooking smells or provide first class beer without serving it in spit and sawdust bars.

Proof that this can be done is provided by the Thunderton House in Elgin, a quite outstanding pub, run by a couple who obviously devoted a good deal of thought to what a good pub should be offering to its customers in the 1980s and then went out and created a pub from scratch, providing everything that a family, a foodie or a beer-swilling, child-hating misogynist could ask for from a pub!

Thunderton House takes its name from Archibald Dunbar of 'Thundertoun', an eighteenth-century owner of the building. It had previously been known as the King's House and the Great Lodging and has a history stretching as far back as the eleventh century, with many associations with Scottish kings. In the fourteenth century it was the palace of Thomas Randolph, Earl of Moray and nephew of Robert the Bruce. The first Lord of Duffus forfeited the house because of his support for the Stuart rebellion of 1715, while in 1746 Lady Arradoul was hostess to Bonnie Prince Charlie there for ten days before the Battle of Culloden. When Lady Arradoul died, his bed sheets were used as her shroud, and his ghost is said to haunt the room in which he slept.

In addition to the ghost of Bonnie Prince Charlie, Thunderton House has a few others; a 'grey lady' who died in childbirth, the father having been killed in the post-Culloden period; a ghost wandering in the conservatory, and a kilted highlander giving the battle cry of Culloden.

Since those times, Thunderton House has been by turns a church, a furniture warehouse, a printers, a masonic lodge, a lemonade factory and a hotel. When Robin and Gay Graham bought it in 1985 it had lain empty for several years and was in a parlous state. They set about restoring it and creating a pub that would fulfil their ideas of the way pubs should be designed and run. They have succeeded magnificently

Sir Harry Lauder's smile provides a welcome for all at Thunderton House

and Thunderton House should be an obligatory calling point for all pub owners, brewery designers and people who like good pubs.

From the start, the Graham's decided that families would not just be tolerated, but catered for and welcomed. There are two entrance doors, one leading into the bar, the other into the family room, which is beautifully fitted out with an open central area surrounded by wood and stained glass partitions. The room is so attractive and comfortable that people without children sometimes have to be ordered out into the main bar to make room for families trying to get in! The Grahams' care and meticulous planning are equally as evident elsewhere – there is a toilet suitable for disabled people and a nappy changing room that can be used by fathers as well as mothers. A father can also take his daughter to the loo without having to hang around waiting for an obliging woman to appear.

Swing doors connect the family room with the main bar, which has a carved wood bar and gantry, stained glass and a high table with brass rail and bar stools. A partitioned area up a couple of steps at the other end of the bar has a stone fireplace and a snuff-taking Highland equivalent of a cigar store Indian. There is a neat and efficient food servery and a lovely conservatory with a stained glass roof. Off the bar are all sorts of interesting nooks and crannies including a narrow bench seat where you can sit and read the newspapers provided by the pub on a reading rack, and a telephone partly enclosed by partitions so that you can make a civilized call even when the pub is busy. Like so many Scottish pubs, Thunderton House has a TV, but it is only switched on for major sporting events.

The beer, from a temperature-controlled cellar, is excellent and there are also over 100 imported beers. There are single malts, as one would expect in a Highland pub, and you can also be sure of a good glass of wine. The Grahams use an American machine which maintains wine at the correct temperature and dispenses it by nitrogen pressure; the nitrogen prevents oxygen reaching the wine and turning it sour, but it is not itself absorbed by wine, so the wine is kept in good condition.

The attention to detail even extends to water, which is dispensed, cooled, from a brass fitting on the bar. Food is available all day; it is extremely good and any item can be supplied in a half-portion on request. Air cleaners extract smoke and food odours from the pub air.

The result of all this is a pub that really does cater for all tastes. Families are made warmly welcome, without intruding on to the bar and spoiling the enjoyment of other people, some of

The snuff-taking Highlander in part of the main bar at Thunderton House

whom may have come to the pub for a bit of peace and quiet away from theirs. The only improvement I would make is to strangle the mechanical parrot in the entrance porch! Though the Graham's have now moved on, the new landlady, Norma Laidlaw, is set to uphold the excellent traditions of Thunderton House.

Leaving Elgin for Inverness, you pass through some beautiful beech woods. Nearby, on the coast, is the village of Findhorn with its famous community, though its bucolic tranquility must be somewhat disturbed by the RAF base at Kinloss nearby. You pass through Forres, still heading west, with the peaks of the Cairngorms rising far to the south.

As you approach the eastern outskirts of Inverness, you will see a sign drawing your attention to one of the most infamous sites in Scottish history: the place where the Duke of Cumberland, 'the butcher of Culloden', put an end to Scots' hopes of independence and the Stuart cause with a massacre of the Highlanders. Stone pyramids along the road mark the sites where the Highlanders buried their dead; Cumberland's losses are marked by a stone with the inscription: 'the English were buried here'. The English 'final solution' to the problem of the Highlands was imposed; the Highland clearances removed much of the surviving population, and, after centuries of war, England and Scotland finally settled into an uneasy peace.

Drive in towards Inverness with the bridge over the Firth arching away to your right. Inverness was the sixth-century capital of the Pictish kingdom. The earliest castle dates from 1141, and Cromwell had the Sconce Fort built here in 1652-7 to control the Highlands. It did not work; Prince James Francis Edward was proclaimed King James VIII in Inverness Castle in 1715, and after the failure of his rebellion, the Jacobites rose again in 1745-6, precipitating their defeat and slaughter at Culloden. Following the battle, the Duke of Cumberland had Inverness castle burned to the ground; the present one is a nineteenth-century creation.

Follow the town centre signs and park in the Eastgate Shopping Centre car park. Walk past the front of the station, which is on Academy Street, and your target, the Phoenix Bar, is further down the street on the right.

The Phoenix' less than imposing exterior, a symphony in shades of drab cream and brown, conceals a public bar that is as authentic an example of the old-fashioned, spit and sawdust Scottish bar as you could wish to meet. The sawdust is still scattered on the floor every day, the spit is mercifully no longer present, but the gutter round the base of the bar

The Phoenix Bar, Inverness – even the bar staff are traditional!

remains. There is a long island bar, some fine etched glass windows, window seats, pine-boarded walls and a few chairs and tables, but basically the Phoenix is a stand-up bar, the sort once widespread in Scotland, but now rare and growing more so. Some will not bemoan the passing of bars that were associated with some of the less savoury aspects of the Scots character, but others will cherish them for their virtues and be willing to forget their vices.

The Phoenix barmen all wear spotless white aprons as they dispense the drinks, with whisky chasers – 'a hauf and a hauf' – very much the order of the day. On my visit the ubiquitous TV was switched on but the sound was turned down; it can be escaped by turning your back on it or going round to the other side of the island bar. The TV is the only false note in a bar full of atmosphere, a relic of the past still well worth visiting in the present.

At the end of a corridor is a lounge bar and food servery with carpets, plush seats and theatre posters on the walls, in strong contrast to the austerity of the public bar. There is live music here on Wednesday to Saturday nights, usually local bands. There is also a small snug with a dartboard where families can go, and which is used for private parties. Food is reasonably priced and always includes a vegetarian dish.

From Inverness we shall now make the long journey south. One route will take you through the Great Glen, following the line of the Caledonian Canal, which runs from Inverness to Fort William on the Atlantic

The Phoenix Bar
Licensee: A. MacBean
106-110 Academy Street, Inverness
☎ Inverness (0463) 233685
11 - 11 (1am Wednesday to Friday; 11.45pm Saturday).

Alice Ale; McEwan 70/-; Younger's No 3

Lunchtime & evening food. Families welcome. Live music Wednesday to Saturday nights.

Sawdust but definitely no spit – the Phoenix Bar at Inverness

coast. Only about one-third of it is actually canal, the rest uses the lochs on the Caledonian fault – Lochy, Oich and, of course, Loch Ness. In summer you can take a boat trip along the canal from Muirtown Locks. Near its western end is Ben Nevis, the highest mountain in Britain, which dominates Fort William, towering 4,406 feet to the south-east of the town. Those who wish to conquer it should take the elementary precautions of wearing the proper clothing and letting someone know where they are going; the weather in the mountains can change with sudden and savage ferocity.

South of Fort William, take the A82 through Glen Coe, scene of yet another infamous massacre, when forty members of the clan MacDonald were slaughtered for their tardiness in declaring allegiance to King William III. On a cold, grey day, Glen Coe seems grim enough to revive memories of that horror; on a fine, sunny day, it is one of the most spectacular sights in Britain. Pass the Bridge of Orchy and drop south beneath the peak of Ben More, then follow the road along the western shore of Loch Lomond, the largest freshwater lake in Britain. It begins in a narrow glen, and finishes in a broad lowland plain, leading you out of the Highlands and down to the Clyde and to Glasgow.

For those in more of a hurry to reach Glasgow, there is a swifter route from Inverness following the A9 past thickly forested hillsides. The road takes you south past Aviemore, the ski capital of Britain, and then in a huge sweep around the Forest of Atholl, through Blair Atholl, seat of the Dukes, with a Disneyland castle, and the Pass of Killiecrankie, yet another battle site, but scene of a rare Scots victory. The road leads on down back to Perth, but this time, follow the A9 south-west through Auchterarder and Dunblane to Stirling, where the castle makes a majestic sight towering 250 feet above the old town.

Stirling was regarded as the key to the Highlands and its vital importance is emphasized by the fifteen battlegrounds that surround the castle. The English were beaten there in 1297 and again in their great defeat in 1314 at Bannockburn, just to the south, following which they made their 'shameful peace' with the Scots. In 1651, General Monck, whose handiwork we have already seen around Inverness, captured the castle for Cromwell, and in 1715 and 1745 the Jacobite advance faltered on their failure to take the castle.

A few miles south of Stirling, pick up the A80 for Glasgow, then take the M8 in towards the city centre. Glasgow's slums, gangs and Gorbals gave it an unenviable reputation with the rest of Britain, but that was always a partial view of what is one of our great cities. Founded by St Mungo in 543, the Gaelic name 'Glas Cau' (green place) is an ironic name for the grimy industrial city it became.

Glasgow became a great trading centre and expanded rapidly in the eighteenth century as the 'Tobacco Lords' made their fortunes on the trade between the Clyde and Virginia. It was in Glasgow that James Watt developed the steam engine in 1769, providing the driving force of the Industrial Revolution. He was the city's chief engineer at the time when the Clyde was opened up from Glasgow to the Firth allowing the development of the great dockyard in the city. The first steamship in the world was launched in Glasgow and the shipyards of the Clyde produced three-quarters of the world's steamships in the nineteenth-century.

Glasgow's phenomenal rate of expansion saw much of the old city torn down. Of the more recent buildings, Charles Rennie Mackintosh's School of Art is an obligatory calling point. Of the few remaining survivals from earlier times, perhaps the most remarkable is St Mungo's Cathedral, one of the only two in Scotland – the other is Kirkwall in Orkney – not to be destroyed either by English soldiers or zealots of the Reformation. The two towers of the west façade were removed by tidy-minded Victorians because they did not match, otherwise the cathedral remains unaltered since its construction between the thirteenth and fifteenth centuries. Next door to it is one of the more remarkable sights of any city, the Necropolis on Fir Park Hill, a burial ground which enabled Glasgow's merchants and industrialists to continue their rivalry into the grave as the 'City of the Dead' sprouted incredible memorials and mausoleums from every era. Mock-Egyptian, Chinese, Greek and Roman tombs rub shoulders with Cecil B. De Mille-style confections; truly one of Britain's great sights!

Glasgow itself has emerged from its mid-century blues and there is an air of great vitality about the city. Glaswegians seem to have rediscovered a sense of pride and purpose, taking their future firmly back into their own hands, and building and re-building are going on all around.

The resolutely traditional Mitre Bar, Glasgow

In Glasgow, as in any other city, the first thing to do is find somewhere to park. George Square is the heart of the city and very close to the two classic Glasgow pubs, but parking there is limited to forty minutes on a meter, so park where you can and use a taxi, bus or the subway, as Glaswegians call the underground. From George Square, leave at the south-east corner, walk east on Ingram Street and then turn into Brunswick Street. Your first target, the Mitre Bar, is to be found at the bottom of the street where it narrows into an alley.

Like the Phoenix Bar in Inverness, the Mitre Bar in Glasgow is resolutely traditional. A central, U-shaped bar has etched glass screens at either end which give some privacy and there are a couple of other nooks and crannies where customers can have private conversations. Otherwise, join the regulars in conversation at the bar and do your best to ignore the TV, which is a permanent and intrusive feature of the Mitre.

Upstairs is a lounge with leatherette seats, copperette-topped tables and a beamette ceiling. Ignore this and stick to the downstairs bar for an unspoilt, no-frills pub with lots of heart and atmosphere.

From the Mitre go on down to the bottom of the street, turn right and walk along Trongate and Argyle Street. Turn right onto Mitchell Street, passing Mackintosh's Glasgow Herald building, and you will find Drury Street off to the left towards the top of the street. Whereas the Mitre is a basic city bar, the Horseshoe is another of the splendid Victorian and Edwardian pubs that grace so many of our industrial cities. From its imposing frontage hang four large lamps and there are lovely stained glass windows, including those brought by the original owner, John Y. White, from his Union Bar on the nearby Union Street.

Inside is a huge banjo-shaped, mahogany bar and a gantry with old spirits barrels inset, dividing the bar into two halves that are almost exact mirror images of each other. There are two horseshoe-shaped fireplaces surmounted by horseshoe-shaped mirrors, tiled murals of the seasons, a mosaic floor, ornate ceiling and heavily carved woodwork around the walls. The mirror images are not confined to the pub's two symmetrical halves, for it also has a fine collection of mirrors, including two of the Horseshoe's own, superbly etched and brilliant cut trademark mirrors.

Brass bell plates ring the walls and there is a remarkable portrait of Queen Victoria, looking far more fat and grumpy than one would have thought prudent for a would-be court painter. She would definitely not have been amused by the likeness.

Around the inside of the woodwork above the bar, whether as inspiration to the staff or to those customers who catch a glimpse, are a string of mottoes, one attributed to Queen Victoria: 'Total abstinence is an impossibility; and it will not do to insist on it as a general practice.' Another, from T.L. Peacock, opines that: 'Not

The Mitre Bar
Licensee: P.R. McCrudden
12 Brunswick Street,
Glasgow
☎ (041) 552 3764
11 - 11 Monday to Saturday.
Closed Sunday.

Belhaven 80/-; Ind Coope
Burton Ale

Lunchtime food. Evening
food until 7.30. Children
over 14 allowed if eating.

The Horseshoe Bar
Licensee: David Smith
17 Drury Street,
Glasgow
☎ (041) 248 4467
11 - midnight (11.30pm
Saturday). Sunday 6.30 - 11

Tennents Heriot 80/-

Lunchtime & evening food.
Families welcome in
upstairs lounge (closed 3 - 5
Monday to Wednesday).

Opposite: Queen Victoria wouldn't like it! The Horseshoe Bar, Glasgow

drunk is he who from the floor can rise alone and still drink more, drunk is he who prostrate lies without the power to drink or rise.' G.S. Calverley provides yet more inspiration with the observation that: 'He that would shine and petrify his tutor should drink Draught Tennents in its Native Pewter.' Students may be well advised not to take this advice too seriously . . .

With or without the doggerel, the Horseshoe is a splendid place to toast the resurgence of Glasgow. The clientele is a mix of business people, students, regulars and visitors who chance on the narrow street in which it stands. Be sure to join them, you will not be disappointed. Upstairs is a lounge and restaurant, but like the Mitre, the place to be is in the downstairs bar – accept no imitations!

Burns' favourite howff – the Globe Inn, Dumfries

There is one more call to make in Scotland, before heading west to Stranraer and the ferry to Belfast, but this involves a long drive south to Dumfries, home of perhaps Scotland's most famous son, Robbie Burns. Take the M8 east to the junction with the M74, which you follow south. After a few miles, it becomes the A74, following the line of a Roman road, connecting the great Roman centre of Carlisle with the Antonine Wall to the north, in the days before the withdrawal to Hadrian's Wall.

Just south of Crawford, turn off onto the A702, also following the line of a Roman road, and drive down through the rolling Border hills to Dumfries. Like almost every important town in Scotland, Dumfries was much fought over by the Scots and English. Edward I took it in 1300, but Robert the Bruce killed the king's emissary, Sir John Comyn, in the Franciscan church there, signalling the rebellion that eventually ended in the defeat of the English at Bannockburn.

The most famous part in the history of Dumfries is played by Robbie Burns, however. The Globe Inn can be found in a narrow winding alley off the High Street and it was described by Burns as 'my favourite howff'. It stands little altered from Burns' time and has much to interest the literary pilgrim.

Burns' 'howff' is the lovely wood-panelled snug, reached through the dining room, its walls lined, like much of the pub, with Burns memorabilia. There is an open fire and to one side of it Burns' favourite chair, still in position. In an upstairs room, two small window panes have Burns' poems in his own hand, engraved with a diamond in the glass. One sings the praises of Polly Stewart, the other contains part of a well-known Burns song 'Gin a body meet a body, coming through the grain'.

Apart from his liking for the warmth and

The Globe Inn
Licensee: J. McKerrow
High Street,
Dumfries
☎ Dumfries (0387) 52335
11 - 11. Sunday 12.30 -
2.30; 6.30 - 11

McEwan 80/-

Food served until 5pm in the restaurant. Families welcome.

The Globe Inn, Dumfries – the only place to be on Burns night

atmosphere of the Globe, something which can be appreciated just as much by a visitor today, Burns had another powerful reason for calling there – the barmaid Helen Ann Park, 'Anna of the Gowden Locks'. Burns had an affair with her and she gave birth to his child. Their relationship is commemorated in Burns' lines:

Yest're'en I had a pint of wine,
A place where body saw na;
Yest're'en lay on this breast o' mine,
The gowden locks o' Anna.

There is an open fireplace in the snug and an iron range in the other dining-room, where families are welcome. There is also a fine, small snug with solid wooden bar and backfittings and wood-panelled walls. The Burns memorabilia includes an etching of his funeral procession through Dumfries in 1797.

There is also a long bar, the stables in Burns' time, with wooden benches and tables. Most of the locals gather there and the conversation and the good humour is right in the Burns tradition. Be there on Burns Night for a night to remember, but call anytime for a bit of the warmth, good humour and history of bonnie Scotland with not a bit of tartan or a sprig of heather in sight!

Six miles south of Dumfries is Sweetheart Abbey, named for Devorguilla Balliol, who kept her husband's embalmed heart in an ivory box for sixteen years so that it and she would be buried together in the abbey she founded in 1273. The rest of its history is less romantic; it was burned down in 1381 and again in 1609, the books, manuscripts and paintings of the abbey being burned in Dumfries market place by the zealots of the Reformation.

To the east across the Solway, where migrant birds in their thousands pause on their way north and south with the seasons, is Carlisle, a town fought over as furiously and frequently as Berwick in the east. Carlisle and its surrounding area were settled with hundreds of loyal Protestant Englishmen to pacify the area, a solution also applied to Belfast, which is our next port of call.

From Dumfries, take the A75 west through Galloway, a particularly beautiful region, which is little known and used by the tourists who swarm eagerly over the Highlands. West of Castle Douglas is Threave Castle, home of the 'Black Douglases'. Above the castle gate is the 'gallows knob' from which some of the Douglases' many enemies were hung. The road runs west through Gatehouse of Fleet and Newton Stewart and on to Stranraer.

Stranraer's value as a port was recognized by the Romans and it has remained a major port through to the present day, the main route for people and goods to Northern Ireland. According to legend the castle foundations were built on bales of wool, to prevent it from sinking into the marshy ground. The warming effects of the Gulf Stream give the whole of south-west Scotland a gentle climate, and the botanic gardens at Logan, a few miles to the south of Stranraer, demonstrate this with a collection of subtropical plants from all over the world.

It is not usually quite so balmy in Belfast, but it does contain possibly the finest example of the High Victorian pub in the United Kingdom, so board the ferry for the short journey across the Irish Sea.

Drinking in the six counties that make up the troubled province of Northern Ireland can be disconcerting. Drinks exist here that will not be found on the mainland. What, for instance, led to the creation of 'brown lemonade' as an alternative to 'white lemonade'? Should either be drunk in combination with the locally renowned McKibbie's Black Rum, which seems descended as much from tarmac as from sugar cane?

The Crown Liquor Saloon is found at the city end of Great Victoria Street opposite the Europa (or Forum) Hotel. This is the beginning of Belfast's 'golden mile', a mixed selection of pubs, clubs, disco bars, hot food carry-outs and ethnic restaurants. A newspaper critic wrote recently that you could buy any kind of food on the golden mile except for a decent meal! It is only the visitors who notice the armoured personnel carriers, the helicopter hovering overhead and the holes in the street façade where the bombed buildings used to be. For all that, you are safer here than in many other cities in Europe.

The Crown is owned by the National Trust and is run by Bass Breweries. In anyone's book this is a world-class drinking establishment. The long granite-top bar is unique in my experi-

The Crown Liquor Saloon
Licensee: Michael Kearney
46 Great Victoria Street, Belfast
☎ Belfast (0232) 249476
11.30 - 11.00.

Lunchtime & evening food.

Perhaps the finest Victorian bar of them all – the Crown Liquor Saloon, Belfast, miraculously unscathed by 'the troubles'

ence, and the bulk of the seating is in 'donkey-boxes': ornately partitioned, private drinking areas seating no more than a dozen people and separated from each other by carved wood and painted glasswork. Wherever the eye alights there is more craftsmanship. The intricately tiled floor, the tinted glass mirrors, the porticoed bar-back and the ebony-stained, moulded plaster ceiling are vivid reminders of a bygone era. The gaslights are real and account for the majority of the pub's illumination.

Catering in Irish pubs tends to be more basic than on the mainland and the Crown's range of pies, soups, sandwiches and stews represents excellent value. Oysters from Strangford Lough may also appear in season.

The biggest omission is the absence of any traditional beer flowing from the banks of ornate handpumps. Bass have been toying for some years with the idea of importing Draught Bass from the mainland and the Crown would seem to be the obvious launching pad for such a move. Meanwhile, make do with the choice of stouts from Guinness or Murphy's.

It is, perhaps, appropriate that this journey round our classic town pubs should end at what is arguably the finest Victorian bar of them all, for the Victorian pub remains a benchmark in how to adapt to changing times without abandoning the traditional virtues.

No doubt there were gnarled old regulars then who grizzled into their porter about the new-fangled snob screens and snugs, as there are those today muttering into their mild as food and family rooms become ever more widespread. Fun pubs and theme pubs will not survive the next twenty years, because they ride roughshod over the history and continuity of pub use, relying instead on ersatz American novelty; they are fast bars, serving fast food and fast drink, and they will disappear fast. No change will ever please all pub-users, but the pubs that will survive little altered from today to delight pub-goers in another hundred years, will be those, like the best Victorian ones, that enrich, rather than ignore, pub tradition.

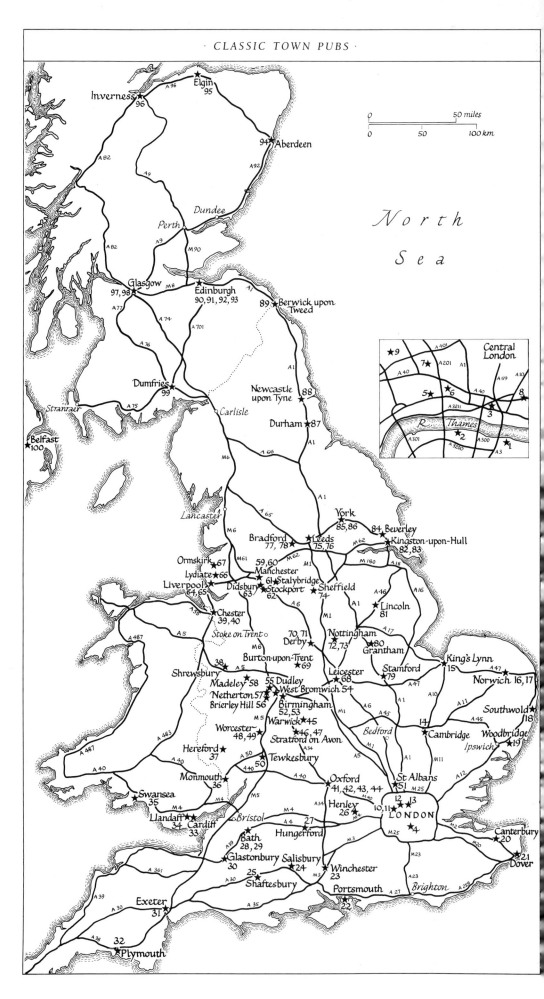

North
Sea

50 miles
0   50   100 km

Central
London
★9
7★
5★ ★6
3
★8
R.   Thames
★2
★1

Inverness ★
96
Elgin
95
★ Aberdeen
94
Dundee
Perth
Glasgow
97,98
Edinburgh
90,91,92,93
89 ★ Berwick upon
Tweed
Dumfries
99
Stranraer
Carlisle
Newcastle
upon Tyne 88
Durham ★87
Belfast
100
Lancaster
York
85,86
84 ★ Beverley
Kingston-upon-Hull
82,83
Bradford
77, 78
Leeds
75,76
Ormskirk ★67
Lydiate ★66
59,60
Manchester
61★ Stalybridge
Liverpool ★
64,65
Didsbury
63
Stockport
62
Sheffield
74
Lincoln
81
Chester
39,40
Stoke on Trent
70, 71
Derby
Nottingham
72,73
★80
Grantham
King's Lynn
15
Shrewsbury
38
Madeley 58
Netherton 57
Brierley Hill 56
55 Dudley
West Bromwich 54
Birmingham
52,53
Burton-upon-Trent
★69
Leicester
★68
Stamford
79
Norwich 16, 17
Southwold
18
Worcester
48,49
Warwick ★45
★46,47
Stratford on Avon
Hereford ★
37
14
Cambridge
Woodbridge
19
Ipswich
Tewkesbury
50
Bedford
Monmouth
36
Oxford
41, 42, 43, 44
St Albans
51
Swansea
35
Henley
26
12 13
10,11
LONDON
4
Canterbury
20
Llandaff ★
34 Cardiff
33
Bristol
Hungerford
Dover
21
Bath
28, 29
Glastonbury
30
25
Shaftesbury
Salisbury
24
Winchester
23
Portsmouth
22
Brighton
Exeter
31
32
Plymouth

INDEX OF PUBS